Wildflowers

OF THE APPALACHIAN TRAIL

SECOND EDITION

OTHER BOOKS BY LEONARD M. ADKINS

Adventure Guide to Virginia

The Appalachian Trail: A Visitor's Companion

Best of the Appalachian Trail: Day Hikes (with Victoria and Frank Logue)

Best of the Appalachian Trail: Overnight Hikes (with Victoria and Frank Logue)

The Caribbean: A Walking and Hiking Guide

50 Hikes in Maryland: Walks, Hikes, and Backpacks from the Allegheny Plateau to the Atlantic Ocean

50 Hikes in Northern Virginia: Walks, Hikes, and Backpacks from the Allegheny Mountains to the Chesapeake Bay

50 Hikes in Southern Virginia: From the Cumberland Gap to the Atlantic Ocean

50 Hikes in West Virginia: From the Allegheny Mountains to the Ohio River

Maryland: An Explorer's Guide

Seashore State Park: A Walking Guide

Walking the Blue Ridge: A Guide to the Trails of the Blue Ridge Parkway

Wildflowers of the Blue Ridge and Great Smoky Mountains (photographer Joe Cook)

Wildflowers

OF THE APPALACHIAN TRAIL

SECOND EDITION

To Phyllis –
Enjoy the flowers!

Leonard M. Adkins

authored by **Leonard M. Adkins**

photographed by **Joe** & **Monica Cook**

Appalachian Trail Conservancy
Harpers Ferry, WV

Menasha Ridge Press
Birmingham, AL

Copyright © 1999, 2006 by Leonard M. Adkins

All rights reserved

Published by Menasha Ridge Press and the Appalachian
  Trail Conservancy

Distributed by The Globe Pequot Press

Printed in Canada

Second Edition/First Printing

Library of Congress Cataloging-in-Publication Data is
available from the Library of Congress.

ISBN 10: 0-89732-974-0

ISBN 13: 978-0-89732-974-3

Cover, text, and cartography by Grant M. Tatum

Photography by Joe & Monica Cook

Photograph of author by Laurie Adkins

Menasha Ridge Press

P. O. Box 43673

Birmingham, AL 35243

www.menasharidge.com

TABLE OF CONTENTS

DEDICATION

For my sister, Kathleen. I am impressed by your life.

Numerous people enthusiastically gave of their time, energy, and expertise. Joe and Monica Cook and I must express our specific appreciation to . . .

Tom Wieboldt, senior laboratory specialist with the Virginia Tech Herbarium; Henning Von Schmelling, horti-culturist with the Chattahoochee Nature Center; and Ann B. Messick, well known in Virginia for the quality of her wildflower slide presentations. These folks willingly went through and referenced well over one hundred photographs to verify the genus and species of each flower. (If there are any errors or omissions of information, the responsibility is ours and not theirs.)

Joe Boyd, Walter E. Daniels, Rachel DuBois, Jan and Bill Eddy, Ted Elliman, Jerry and Mary Hopson, Ralph H. Kinter, Patty Lowe, Paul A. Palmer, Ginny Smith, and Ray Welch provided us with firsthand information (based on field observations) regarding the trail locations of many of the individual species. Kent Schwarzkopf with the National Park Service and Sarah Evans of the Maine Natural Areas Division supplied additional data.

Dr. Stephen Lewis, Caroline Charonko, Terri, and Susie—I would never have experienced all of the beauty I have if you had not come to my rescue.

Nancy Adkins—How did I luck out and get you for my mother?

Laurie—My one and only trailmate.

ACKNOWLEDGMENTS

We must provide enough wilderness areas so that, no matter how dense our population, man—though apartment born—may attend the great school of the outdoors, and come to know the joys of walking the woods . . . Once he experiences that joy, he will be restless to return over and over again . . . If that is to happen, the places where the goldthread, monkey flower, spring beauty, or starflower flourish in sphagnum moss must be made as sacred as any of our shrines.

~ William O. Douglas

It has been nearly two decades since I first set foot on the Appalachian Trail. As I stepped forth from Springer Mountain, Georgia, on that early spring day, I was ready to revel in the grand scenery of the mountains, the far-off vistas, the roaring waterfalls, the crimson-gold sunsets. I might occasionally stop to taste a wild strawberry or enjoy a particularly beautiful blossom, but I had little interest in the world at my feet and could have counted all the flowers I knew by name on the fingers of my hands.

Yet, as the miles drew me northward, I could not ignore the attractive pink petals of Spring Beauty flowers delivering the promise of warmer days to come. It seemed everywhere I looked tiny Bluets spread out in lengthy carpets along the edges of the trail, mirroring the clarity of the sky above me, while Flame Azalea reflected the sunsets of which I was so fond. How could I have been so ignorant of such an exquisite element of the Appalachian Trail? How could I have always been questing after the big picture, while overlooking the smaller elements that make up the whole? It was time to learn more about this natural world of which I was becoming a part.

INTRODUCTION

The Appalachian Trail (AT) winds for more than 2,100 miles through the mountains from Georgia to Maine. Along the way it traverses lofty ridgelines, wanders into hidden hillside coves, courses through river valleys dotted with farmlands, and even makes contact with the artificial world of human communities. In other words, it touches upon nearly every environment to be found in the Appalachian Mountains. This variety of latitudes, elevations, and settings means that visitors to the trail—be they casual walkers, day hikers, weekenders, or long-distance travelers—have the opportunity to discover the beauty that comes from the grand diversity of flowers to be found along the way.

The hardest aspect of putting this book together was deciding which of the many Appalachian Mountain flowers to include and which to exclude. So that this book could be as specific to the trail as possible, the Cooks and I decided to begin with a list of the more than one hundred flowers that are mentioned in the official trail guides available from the Appalachian Trail Conservancy. Dropped from the list were a number of species that were related and quite similar to each other, while a few species we felt were common were added. In addition, a couple of species that are quite rare, and therefore of great interest, were also included.

The result is a volume comprising more than one hundred photographs, with detailed descriptions and background information on ninety-four species. There are also citations of more than sixty additional species with respect to their distinguishing features.

As you use this book, please take this admonishment to heart: Do not pick, dig, harvest, or disturb any flowers you find growing in the wild! Such activity is illegal along a large percentage of the AT, and the natural world is having a hard enough time coping with the changes that modern civilization has brought to our planet. Leave the plants where they are so that they may propagate themselves and live out their lives in their native surroundings.

As I stated in one of my other books, *The Appalachian Trail: A Visitor's Companion*, the longer I study the environment of the trail, the more convinced I become that its greatest importance—much more than the recreational opportunities it provides—is its preservation of the natural world from the encroachments and destructions of our society. It is this that I firmly believe our descendants will look upon as the true value and legacy of the AT.

When I first conceived of *Wildflowers of the Appalachian Trail*, I wanted it to be a work of visual art as well as a reference guide. I wanted the photographs to capture the beauty of the flowers and of the natural world of the AT. I knew the photographers I wanted—Joe and Monica Cook—and they have not disappointed me. They spent two full hiking seasons traveling up and down the trail in order to be at the right place at the right time to catch a particular plant in bloom. Their photographs have made the book as appropriate for display on a coffee table as for use in the field.

Some people will advise you to hike with binoculars so you can enjoy the grandeur of the mountain vistas; I would urge you to bring along a small magnifying glass as well—so you can better appreciate the delicate and intricate features of the flowers. May this book lead you to many wonderful hours of discovery on the AT, to a new fascination with the intricate workings of the natural world, and to a renewed sense of delight for the simple, yet elegant beauty of a flower. Happy trails!

~ Leonard M. Adkins

HOW TO USE THIS BOOK

Because coloration is one of the most distinguishing aspects of a wildflower, I have arranged the flowers in this book in five groups according to flower color—white, yellow to orange, pink to red, violet to blue, and green. If a flower has more than one color (such as Painted Trillium, which is white with pink highlights), it is placed within the grouping of its most predominant color. If a flower may bloom in different colors (for instance, the Round-Lobed Hepatica can produce white, pink, lilac, or even lavender-blue blossoms), it is put into the color that is most common, and mention is made of the variant colors.

Within each color group, the plants are arranged in the order of their flowering. So, a flower that appears in March has been placed before one that blooms in April. Where two plants bloom in the same month, the one that stops blooming earlier has been placed in front of the plant that blooms for the longer period.

Many wildflowers have more than one common name, and each of those names may or may not be recognized throughout its entire range. For example, Trout Lily is variously known as Dogtooth Violet, Adder's-Tongue, and Fawn Lily. To identify a flower, I have used what I believe to be the name most widely used along the length of the trail. Other common names are cited within the body of the text, but it is entirely possible that your own research may lead you to discover additional ones.

This confusion over common names was the impetus for Swedish botanist Carl Linnaeus to establish a scientific system of names in the 1700s. Using Latin and Greek words as a base, he identified plants and animals with a genus name (always capitalized) followed by a species name (in lowercase.) Thus, no matter how the Trout Lily was known locally, it could be referred to worldwide as *Erythronium americanum*.

For the most part this works well, but you will sometimes find that scientific names do not always agree in various reference books. Scholars have long held to the rule that the first published name of a plant (accompanied by a well-founded description) becomes its scientific name. Yet, further research into a plant's true characteristics often requires a change in the name. I've tried to note such name changes in the text of this book.

Because the scientific names given in *Gray's Manual of Botany* are the ones most often referenced by the majority of popular flower guides in use today—such as *Peterson's*, *Newcombs'*, and the *National Audubon Society Field Guide*—I also use those names. However, some sources have elected to employ the scientific names of plants as listed in *A Synonymized Checklist of the Vascular Flora of the United States, Canada, and Greenland* by John T. Kartesz. I have noted in the body of the text when the names used by Kartesz are different than those of Gray.

Information on each plant is divided into the following key sections:

- The FLOWER section provides a succinct description of the plant's blossom, giving a general overview of its size, color, shape, and any other distinguishing characteristics.

- The BLOOM SEASON provides the plant's overall maximum flowering time limits. In its 2,100 miles from Georgia to Maine, the AT winds through a wide variety of habitats and elevations, making it hard to say exactly when you will find a certain flower in bloom in a certain place. In other words, "March to June" may mean that blooms which appear on a plant in March in lower elevations or in the southern part of its range might have disappeared by the time the blossoms of the same species arrive in June along the northern portion of the AT or at higher elevations.

- A description of the plant's leaves and of its average height is found in the LEAVES AND STEM section.

- The RANGE gives a broad overview of where the plant may be found. Do keep in mind that it may or may not be found along the AT in every state within its range, but that it is known to inhabit the (wide) general vicinity of the trail in those states.

- Because guides which just identify flowers tend to be dry and boring, interesting tidbits about each flower—such as its reproduction or survival, its reputed medicinal uses, folklore on how it received its name, data on related species, or information relating the plant directly to the AT—have been included as well.

- One of this book's most distinctive features is that it identifies several places along the trail where you are most likely to encounter each flower. Bear in mind that the word is *likely*—not *guaranteed*. Many factors, such as wind, amount of precipitation, temperature, or disturbances to its environment, go into determining how profusely—if at all—a plant will bloom, or whether it will continue to grow in the same place. To help you find the locations cited, each site mentioned can be found in the index of its respective Appalachian Trail Guide, available from the Appalachian Trail Conservancy. (Information on the Great Smoky Mountains National Park may be found in both the North Carolina–Georgia and the Tennessee–North Carolina guides.)

Here again, Joe, Monica, and I feel the need to reiterate and reinforce what was said earlier: once you have found the flowers, please do not pick, dig, harvest, or disturb them in any way. Several of them are rare or endangered and are becoming more so with each passing day.

If you are interested in growing wildflowers, you can obtain a list of nurseries that propagate them from seeds and cuttings by writing the North Carolina Botanical Gardens, University of North Carolina, Totten Center, Chapel Hill, North Carolina 27599-3375; www.ncbg.unc.edu.

You should also be aware that the Appalachian Trail Conservancy is the umbrella association that oversees and coordinates the efforts to build, maintain, and protect the trail and its surrounding lands. Those of you who hike or have an interest in the AT owe it to yourselves to join this effective organization:

Appalachian Trail Conservancy

P. O. Box 807

Harpers Ferry, WV 25425

304.535.6331

www.appalachiantrail.org

Wildflowers

BLOODROOT

Sanguinaria canadensis

FLOWER:

The one- to two-inch blossom has eight or more white to pinkish petals around a cluster of many sepals.

BLOOM SEASON:

March to May

LEAVES AND STEM:

A single, five- to nine-lobed leaf enfolds the stem when it first appears but opens fully after the flower has bloomed. Persists into late summer.

RANGE:

Georgia to Maine

Bloodroot's name comes from the red or orange sap that flows freely whenever its stem or root is cut or broken. Its other common name of Red Puccoon is derived from the Native American word *pak*, meaning "blood." These earliest inhabitants of North America used the sap as an insect repellent, a treatment for rheumatism and ringworm, and a dye for clothing, baskets, and facial paint.

Like all members of the Poppy family, Bloodroot's juice is toxic, so early settlers were taking quite a chance when they put drops of it on a lump of sugar to treat coughs. The plant also contains the alkaloid sanguinarine, which appears to have anticancer properties and has been used as an anesthetic, an antiseptic, and an antiplaque agent in toothpastes and mouthwashes.

Because the plant must endure the cold temperatures of early spring, the leaves stay curled around the stems to conserve warmth and do not fully expand until pollination occurs. Since insects so vital to the pollination process are scarce at this time of year, the Bloodroot flower—which usually only lasts two to four days—has developed the ability to produce copious amounts of pollen. This helps ensure self-pollination if no insects happen by. To protect its reproductive parts, the flower closes up at night until pollination does occur. Within two to three weeks of that event, light green pods appear, which eventually split open and release the seeds for dispersal.

Some places along the AT you are likely to encounter Bloodroot: Between Springer Mountain and Neel's Gap in Georgia; on the mountains along the North Carolina–Tennessee border; between High Rocks and Spivey Gap in North Carolina; south of the New River in southwest Virginia; on Tar Jacket Ridge, Thunder Ridge, and in Petites Gap in central Virginia; throughout Shenandoah National Park; between the Hudson River and Canopus Lake in New York; and south of Ten Mile River in Connecticut.

RUE ANEMONE

Anemonella thalictroides

With one to three blossoms rising from the main stem, the one-inch-wide flowers have five to ten, white to pinkish sepals.

March to May

A pair, or sometimes a whorl, of one-inch, ovate leaves are divided into three lobes and situated below the blossom. A set of basal leaves usually appear on the four- to eight-inch-high stem once the plant has stopped blooming.

Georgia to Maine

A member of the Buttercup family and found in the open woodlands along the AT, Rue Anemone's long, thin stems tremble in the slightest of winds—prompting its other common name, Windflower. Drawing upon this characteristic, its genus name honors the Greek god of wind, Anemos, who used the flowers as harbingers of spring. Another legend states that these flowers developed from the goddess of love, Venus, when her tears fell upon the ground as she wept over the death of Adonis, her lover.

Certain ancient peoples believed wind that had passed over a field of Anemones was poisoned; the Persians even designated the flower as an emblem of illness. Because it grew well throughout the countryside in Palestine, Christians came to believe Christ spoke of one of the Rue Anemone's relatives, the Poppy Anemone (*Anemone coronaria;* not found along the AT), when he said, "Consider the lilies of the field . . ."

Another relative, False Rue Anemone (*Isopyrum biternatum*), has basically the same AT range and resembles Rue Anemone, but its alternate leaves are divided into three or nine, three-lobed leaflets. In addition, Rue Anemone is often found growing around the roots of trees, intermixed with the blossoms of the Wood Anemone (*Anemone quinquefolia;* see page 22).

When looking to other sources for further information about Rue Anemone, you should be aware that some reference books follow the classifications of John T. Kartesz and list the plant as *Thalictrum thalictroides.*

Some places along the AT you are likely to encounter Anemones: On Max Patch in North Carolina; on Humpback Mountain in central Virginia; throughout Shenandoah National Park; from US 522 to Virginia 55 in northern Virginia; near Silver Hill Campsite and Undermountain Road in Connecticut; and in meadows between Stony Brook Shelter and Norwich in Vermont.

TRAILING ARBUTUS

Epigaea repens

FLOWER:

The white to pink flowers—which grow in little clusters from the ends of the stem or out of the leaf axils— are only about half an inch long, have five spreading lobes, and are well known for their strong fragrance.

BLOOM SEASON:

March to early June

LEAVES AND STEM:

This is a trailing shrub whose woody stems are covered with fine hairs. The alternate, oblong, leathery leaves remain green throughout the year.

RANGE:

Georgia to Maine

As you huff and puff up a steep grade along a rocky hillside in late winter or early spring, you may notice that the air you are sucking in to provide the much-needed oxygen for your calf muscles suddenly becomes laden with a most wonderful perfume. It is time to drop your pack, take a break, and search for the source of this olfactory pleasure.

This Lilliputian flower's delightful scent almost led to its demise. In the early part of the twentieth century it was so highly prized for floral bouquets that commercial diggers nearly wiped out the country's entire native population. Unto this day it remains protected by law in many states in hopes it will reestablish itself. Its sensitivity to disturbances by human activity, such as roadbuilding, logging, agriculture, or housing development, only exacerbates the problem.

Where it does grow, Trailing Arbutus sometimes forms dense mats, thanks to its horizontally creeping woody stems. You may have to get down on hands and knees, brush away some forest litter, and lift up the evergreen leaves of the Trailing Arbutus in order to finally see its blossom. For the most part, the flowers are unisexual, with the males growing on separate stems and having a bit of a yellowish hue. It is believed that queen bumblebees, which are among the first insects to emerge in the early spring, are the plant's chief pollinators. In a process known as *myrmecochory*, ants—which are attracted to a sticky substance on the outside of the capsule—provide a significant link in the dispersal of the seeds. See Wood Anemone (*Anemone quinquefolia; see* page 22) for a detailed description of this process.

Some places along the AT you are likely to encounter Trailing Arbutus: Between Deep Gap and Wallace Gap, and between Deer Park Mountain Shelter and Hot Springs in North Carolina; in the James River Face Wilderness and between Johns Hollow and Rocky Row Run in central Virginia; just north of the Undermountain Trail junction in Connecticut; and along Sherman Brook in Massachusetts.

STAR CHICKWEED

Stellaria pubera

FLOWER:
The five petals of the one-half-inch white flowers are so deeply cleft that they appear to have ten petals. Ten stamens rise above the petals in a ring.

BLOOM SEASON:
March to June

LEAVES AND STEM:
The oblong, three-leaves grow stalkless on the upper part of the six- to sixteen-inch stem, while the lower leaves may have long stalks. The stems of the Star Chickweed have many weak, almost translucent branches with vertical lines of tiny hairs.

RANGE:
Georgia to New Jersey

Although it is now most appreciated for the beauty of its flower, Star Chickweed has been of great value through the centuries to birds, animals, and humans. Several species of birds find its seeds to be quite delectable (which accounts for one of its other common names, Birdseed), while grazing animals are drawn to it for its rich copper content. The plant can still be found for sale in the early spring in some markets of Europe; when picked before the flowers develop, it is considered to be more tender than many other wild greens. Its raw leaves are added to salads and, when boiled, taste like fresh-cooked spinach. Because it is high in vitamins A and C, Star Chickweed has been helpful in the treatment of scurvy. It has also been used as a poultice for abscesses and boils, and some people believe that bathing in water in which it has been boiled will reduce swelling.

While on the trail, you can use the Star Chickweed to help you predict the weather. According to folklore, the sun will be shining bright if the blossoms are spread out to their fullest. If they begin to close up, you had better get out the raingear, as precipitation will begin to fall within the next few hours.

Somewhat similar in appearance, Common Chickweed (*Stellaria media*) is found from Georgia to Maine, but its petals are shorter than its sepals—the opposite of Star Chickweed. Mouse-ear Chickweed (*Cerastium vulgatum*) has hairy, oval, sessile leaves that resemble mouse ears and a stem that is covered by sticky hairs. The petals and sepals of its flowers are about equal in length.

Some places along the AT you are likely to encounter one of the Chickweeds: At the base of Amicalola Falls on the AT approach trail in Georgia; north of Angel's Rest in southwest Virginia; on the side trail to Sunset field and on The Priest in central Virginia; and south of Pocosin fire Road in Shenandoah National Park.

PLANTAIN-LEAVED PUSSYTOES

Antennaria plantaginifolia

FLOWER:

The small white flowers of the Plantain-Leaved Pussytoes grow in a terminal cluster of fuzzy flower-heads. Female flowers may look a bit pink, while male flowers (which are rarer) are slightly smaller and have a dusting of brown pollen on their tips.

BLOOM SEASON:

Late March to June

LEAVES AND STEM:

The most noticeable leaves are the basal ones which grow on long stalks and are spoon-shaped with several distinctive veins. Growing along the six- to eighteen-inch stem may be a few lanceolate leaves.

RANGE:

Georgia to Maine

Just one look at Pussytoes is enough to let you recognize how the plants received their common name. The cluster of flowers look like the bottom of a cat's paw, and the tiny petals and hairs emanating from them are reminiscent of a kitten's soft fur.

The flowers, which AT hikers may encounter from Georgia to Maine, are often found flourishing by themselves in large communities along the trail. Not only does the plant favor poorer soils in which many other types of vegetation cannot grow, but like similar foliage found in arid places, it releases a substance that other plants find objectionable, thereby precluding them from growing alongside the Pussytoes.

There is disagreement among botanists as to just exactly how many species of Pussytoes exist. Some experts say the number is no more than six, while others who have studied the plants say there are more than thirty different species. Although it is easy to recognize a plant as Pussytoes, it is hard to distinguish between the many different species.

In addition to Plantain-Leaved Pussytoes, you may find Field Pussytoes (*Antennaria neglecta*) inhabiting the trail environment. This species is usually smaller and its narrower basal leaves will have only one vein. Ranging from Virginia to New England, the leaves of the Smaller Pussytoes (*Antennaria neodioica*) also only have one main vein, while the Solitary Pussytoes (*Antennaria solitaria*), found from Georgia to Maryland/Pennsylvania, have only one flower-head.

Some places along the AT you are likely to encounter one of the Pussytoes: Woody Gap in Georgia; and close to Jennings Creek and south of the Bryant Ridge Shelter in central Virginia.

SERVICEBERRY

Amelanchier arborea

There are so many kinds of Serviceberries that there is still conjecture in the scientific community as to just how many species of *Amelanchier* actually exist in the world. Although the genus is easily recognized, the variations between the species are so slight that positive identification is often next to impossible. Cross-pollination and hybridization only compound the problem. A member of the Rose family, Serviceberry is also variously known as Sarvisberry, Shadbush, and Juneberry. Most Serviceberries are large shrubs, but some—like the *Amelanchier arborea*—can reach heights nearing forty feet. The plants are at their most striking in early spring when they are adding large splashes of white to otherwise still winter-dull hillsides. Later the Serviceberries' clusters of flowers are accentuated and set off nicely by the deep, rich, purple blossoms covering almost every inch of neighboring Redbud trees (which range from Georgia to Connecticut).

In early summer, the Serviceberry's flowers give way to reddish-purple berries one-half inch in diameter—a favorite food of ruffed grouses, wild turkeys, deer, bears, raccoons, and other wildlife. At one time the fruits were widely harvested and eaten fresh or cooked into puddings, pies, and preserves. The Cree Indians made a long-lasting pemmican by mixing the dried berries with cured meat and animal fat. Unknowingly, most hikers today overlook this very sweet treat that nature provides, often within an arm's reach of the trail.

Some places along the AT you are likely to encounter one of the Serviceberries: Between Indian Gap and Newfound Gap in the Great Smoky Mountains National Park on the North Carolina–Tennessee border; along Catawba Mountain and south of Rocky Row Run in central Virginia; between Sages Ravine and Bear Rock Falls, and on Mount Greylock in Massachusetts; and south of Flagstaff Road in Maine.

DUTCHMAN'S-BREECHES

Dicentra cucullaria

Living up to its name, this uncommonly-shaped, three-quarter-inch, waxy flower looks like an upside-down pair of white, puffy pants. The outer two of its four petals have spurs which form a V, while the inner two have tips that are somewhat spoon-shaped. Several droop in a row from a single, arched stem.

April to May

The three- to six-inch leaves are compound and grow upright on long stalks, which are attached to stems that may reach a height of twelve inches.

Georgia to Maine

By far one of the most enjoyable flowers to come across while hiking, the fragrant Dutchman's-Breeches favors the AT's rocky hillsides (usually the north slope), rich woods, and stream banks, and is often found alongside Spring Beauty (*Claytonia virginica;* see page 128) and Trout Lily (*Erythronium americanum;* see page 94). Its perfume and unique shape are natural attractants to bumblebees and honeybees. Though these insects are the main instruments of cross-fertilization for the flower, some are not justly rewarded for their work. The feet of the honeybees pick up the pollen, but their short tongues are unable to reach the nectar. It is believed, however, that the longer proboscises of the bumblebees enable them to enjoy the flower's sweet juices.

Grazing animals, such as cattle, are also attracted to Dutchman's-Breeches, but they may pay a price for their browsing. The plant is poisonous, containing alkaloids that act as a depressant to the central nervous system. Within a couple of days of ingesting the plant, an animal will begin to stumble, shake, and labor to breathe, and it may face death.

Under proper preparation, however, the plant's properties have been used beneficially. Veterinarians administer it to anesthetize large animals, and its bulb has been dried and used as a tonic and blood purifier.

Related species commonly seen along the AT include Wild Bleeding Heart (*Dicentra eximia*; see page 196) and Squirrel Corn (*Dicentra canadensis*; see page 196).

Some places along the AT you are likely to encounter members of the genus *Dicentra:* Between Indian Gap and Newfound Gap in Great Smoky Mountains National Park; on Bluff Mountain along the North Carolina–Tennessee border; between Max Patch and Roaring Fork Shelter in North Carolina; on the north side of Pearis Mountain in southwest Virginia; between the James River and Punchbowl Mountain in central Virginia; in low areas of Shenandoah National Park; and just north of Fernside Road in Massachusetts.

WOOD ANEMONE

Anemone quinquefolia

Wood Anemone has no petals; its solitary flower contains four to nine, white (sometimes pink on the underside), petal-like sepals and numerous stamens and pistils.

April to June

The basal leaves are deeply toothed and divided into three to five leaflets; similar upper leaves grow in a whorl of three near the summit of the four- to eight-inch-high stem.

Georgia to Maine

Growing from Georgia to Maine, and often found clustered around the roots of trees intermixed with Rue Anemone (*Anemonella thalictroides;* see page 10), the Wood Anemone is an early spring flower. Like a number of flowers that bloom as this time of year, ants help disseminate the Wood Anemone's seeds. Attracted to oils and possibly other nutrients found in the bulges—known as elaiosomes—on the plant's seed casing, the ants bring the casings back to their tunnels and eat the elaiosomes. Because the rest of the casing is too hard to open, the ants discard the seed—which is then able to geminate and sprout within the safety of the tunnel. Among the other woodland flowers which are aided by this process—known to botanists as *myrmecochory* (meaning ant farming)—are Wild Ginger (*Asarum canadense;* see page 170), Trailing Arbutus (*Epigaea repens;* see page 12), Bloodroot (*Sanguinaria canadenis;* see page 8), Round-Lobed Hepatica (*Hepatica americana;* see page 126), and the Trilliums (genus *Trillium;* see pages 34–37 and 196–197).

Because the Wood Anemone blooms early in the spring when the number of bees and insects is often low, the plant depends upon the wind to shake loose its pollen and spread it to nearby flowers. Once pollination occurs, the sepals fall off and a hairy, seedlike fruit develops. Soon afterwards, the leaves die back and all aboveground signs of the plant disappear.

Some authorities comment that the plant's name comes from the pairing of the word *anemos* (meaning "wind") with *mone* (which means "habitat"), pointing out that the flower grows in windy areas and at the windiest time of the year.

Some places along the AT you are likely to encounter Anemones: Between Indian Gap and Newfound Gap in the Great Smoky Mountains National Park; between Thornton Gap and Gravel Springs Gap in Shenandoah National Park; and between Lions Head and Bear Mountain in Connecticut.

FOAMFLOWER

Tiarella cordifolia

FLOWER:
The small, quarter-inch, white flowers grow in clusters at the end of a usually leafless, six- to twelve-inch raceme. Each flower has five tapering petals and ten very long, very conspicuous stamens tipped with orange or red anthers.

BLOOM SEASON:
April to June

LEAVES AND STEM:
Growing on long stalks, the two- to four-inch basal leaves are round to heart-shaped. Sharply toothed edges and three to seven shallow lobes make each leaf resemble a maple leaf. The upper surfaces are hairy, while the undersides may be smooth or slightly downy. The plant rises on a stem that can reach close to one foot in height.

RANGE:
Georgia to Maine

Spreading by underground runners to form small colonies that provide excellent ground cover to prevent erosion, Foamflower favors rich woodlands, the disturbed soil along side trails, and the environments found around shaded mountain streams.

As you approach them from a distance, the flowers and their lacy stamens have a tendency to look like frothy foam balanced on the end of a long stem. This explains the common name, but several different sources give slightly varying accounts as to how the plant received its genus name of *Tiarella*, which means "little tiara." Some say the yellow pistils rising above the white petals resembles the points of a golden crown—referred to by the Greeks as a tiara. Other sources claim the generic name refers to the headdress once worn by Persians, as the shape of the pistils resembles a turban. In her excellent study, *The Woman's Day Book of Wildflowers*, Jean Hersey states that the name is in reference to the seed capsule, which is cloven, or split, like a tiara.

Foamflower is also commonly called False Miterwort because of its resemblance to the Miterworts. The Two-Leaf Miterwort (*Mitella diphylla*), ranging from Georgia to southern New England, has a pair of stalkless, heart-shaped leaves which grow on the stem just below a cluster of small, finely fringed, star-shaped flowers. The basal leaves have stalks and are sort of egg-shaped. Found from Pennsylvania to New England, Naked Miterwort (*Mitella nuda*) is smaller and lacks the leaves just below the flowers.

Some places along the AT you are likely to encounter Foamflower: South of the Nantahala River, and between High Rocks and Spivey Gap in North Carolina; close to Fernside Road in Massachusetts; and between Beamis Stream and South Pond in Maine.

MAYAPPLE

Podophyllum peltatum

Mayapple makes its appearance in March, about the same time Bloodroot (*Sanguinaria canadensis;* see page 8) is blooming. Wrapped tightly around the stem when the plant is pushing its way out of the ground, the umbrella-like leaves soon open up to form huge carpets spreading out across much of the forest floor around the AT.

In the past this plant was used as a treatment for warts, but even today chemicals found in Mayapple are used for medicinal purposes—podophyllin is used as a purgative and, along with peltatine, has been employed for the treatment of cancer and venereal disorders. Researchers have found that the latter substance affects DNA and RNA synthesis and discourages the growth of cells.

Despite its name, the fruit, which looks more like a yellowish-green, egg-shaped berry than an apple, does not begin to develop until mid- to late summer. Many people think it has a disagreeable odor when it first appears, but its scent becomes more pleasant as it ripens. Comments from those who have eaten the fruit range from "like a sweet lemon" to "tasteless" to "nauseating." Euell Gibbons felt that a bit of Mayapple juice squeezed into lemonade improved the drink's flavor, and some hikers have been known to use the juice to help mask the taste of iodine-purified water. Just be careful if you decide to do so; the apple is known to be a strong (and quick-acting!) laxative, and other parts of the plant contain a toxic poison that Native Americans are said to have used to commit suicide.

Some places along the AT you are likely to encounter Mayapple: Between Neels Gap and Unicoi Gap in Georgia; near Spring Mountain Shelter on the North Carolina–Tennessee border; between High Rocks and Spivey Gap in North Carolina; between Grassy Ridge and Yellow Mountain Gap on the North Carolina–Tennessee border; Pearis Mountain in southwest Virginia; and Thunder Ridge and Humpback Mountain in central Virginia.

WILD STONECROP

Sedum ternatum

FLOWER:
   Arranged in a floral spray usually along three often-curving horizontal branches, the half-inch-wide, star-shaped flowers have five, white, narrow-pointed petals, ten stamens with dark anthers, and several green sepals.

BLOOM SEASON:
   April to June

LEAVES AND STEM:
   The round to spoon-shaped leaves are smooth, thick, and grow in whorls of three on the portion of the stem that creeps along the ground. The leaves on the upper part of the stem, which rises toward the floral sprays, grow singly. A number of leaf bracts appear just below the petals of the flowers.

RANGE:
   Georgia to New York

Wild Stonecrop has stems that creep along the ground and over boulders, often forming large colonies along stream-banks, in moist woods, and on large rocks (especially limestone). Like cactus, it is a succulent—meaning it has fleshy tissues designed to conserve water. Quite a hardy plant, it is able to endure harsher growing conditions than many other plants found in the Appalachian Mountains.

Not a native of North America, Wild Stonecrop was imported from Europe because of its medicinal uses. Some people used parts of the plant to treat warts and skin sores, while others found it to be an effective diuretic.

The whorl of three leaves gave the plant its species name of *ternatum*, which means "coming together in threes," while the genus name of *Sedum* is derived from a word meaning "to sit," and refers to the way the plant perches itself on rocks, boulders, and logs.

A relative found ranging from North Carolina to Maine, Mossy Stonecrop (*Sedum acre*) has stems that are covered by small, thick leaves of about a quarter-inch in length. Mossy Stonecrop's other common name, Wallpepper, comes from the fact that it likes to climb garden walls and that its leaves have a bit of a peppery taste.

Some places along the AT you are likely to encounter one of the Stonecrops: On the rock walls found in Great Smoky Mountains National Park on the North Carolina–Tennessee border; between Big Horse Gap and Sugar Run Gap, and on the north slope of Pearis Mountain in southwest Virginia; and on Tinker Cliffs and Humpback Mountain in central Virginia.

CUT-LEAVED TOOTHWORT

Dentaria laciniata

Growing in a cluster at the end of an erect stem, Cut-Leaved Toothwort's white to pink flowers consist of four petals in the form of a cross.

April to June

A whorl of three leaves, each divided into three narrow lobes, grows about halfway up a stem eight to fifteen inches high; basal leaves (often absent when the plant is blooming) are upright.

Georgia to Vermont

Favoring rich, moist woodlands, and often found growing in bottomlands beside creeks and streams, the rootstock of the Cut-Leaved Toothwort has a peppery, almost horseradish-type taste. For this reason, the root was often chopped and added as a spice to soups and salads. Just nibbling on it will give you an idea of its flavoring.

A relative, the Slender Toothwort (*Dentaria heterophylla*), has similar leaves, but it has only two leaves (toothed or un-toothed), which are narrower and smaller. The long-stemmed basal leaves are divided into three broad leaflets, and the flowers range from white to pale purple. Two-Leaved Toothwort (*Dentaria diphylla*), also commonly called Pepper-wort, grows between North Carolina and Maine. Although its flowers are similar to the Cut-Leaved Toothwort, it has a pair of opposite stem leaves, each divided into three very broad, toothed lobes. The basal leaves have longer stalks and are almost egg-shaped. Another relative, the Large Toothwort (*Dentaria maxima*), has similar leaves to the Pepperwort, but it's three leaves emanate from the stem at widely spaced intervals instead of appearing as pairs of opposite leaves.

The Toothworts received their common and genus names from the toothlike projections found on their under-ground stems and rootstocks. Because of this, the Doctrine of Signatures (a belief that a plant can cure the ailing body part it resembles) held that the plants would relieve the pain of a toothache. You should be aware that *Gray's Manual of Botany* lists these plants as *Dentaria*, while *A Synonymized Checklist of the Vascular Flora of the United States, Canada, and Greenland* by Kartesz lists them as *Cardamine*.

Some places along the AT you are likely to encounter one of the Toothworts: Between Neels Gap and Unicoi Gap in Georgia; on Tar Jacket Ridge in central Virginia; south of Pocosin Hollow and in low areas of Shenandoah National Park; between US 522 and VA 55 in northern Virginia; and on the south side of Mount Grelock in Massachusetts.

WHITE FRINGED PHACELIA

Phacelia fimbriata

FLOWER:

Appearing in clusters, the individual, half-inch-in-diameter flowers have five petals that are so deeply and finely fringed that they seem to be festooned with thick hairs. The petals range from light blue to lavender to white, while the anthers are lilac.

BLOOM SEASON:

April to June

LEAVES AND STEM:

The two-inch-long, oblong leaves are arranged alternately on a sometimes hairy stem that may reach more than a foot in height. With five to eleven lobes, the upper leaves have no stalks while the basal ones do.

RANGE:

Georgia to Virginia/West Virginia

There are some places in the woods where White Fringed Phacelia, a decidedly southern plant, grows in such abundantly large colonies that entire hillsides look as if someone has come along and spread confetti throughout the forest. Looking closely at the flower—best done with a magnifying glass—reveals tiny, but deep, fringes (in botanical terms, fimbrations) around the blossoms' outer edges, which provide the flower with an overall soft and feathery look.

Not quite as common along the Appalachian Trail as White Fringed Phacelia, Miami Mist (*Phacelia purshii;* see page 196) is quite similar. Ranging from Georgia to Pennsylvania, its blossoms have a bit of blue along the outer edges and are a yellowish green toward the center. Also ranging from Georgia to Pennsylvania—and quite similar to its other two relatives—is the Small-Flowered Phacelia (*Phacelia dubia*). Its flowers, which first appear in a coil but straighten out as the plant develops, are smaller in size and have no fringes along the outer edge of the petals.

The Phacelias are all members of the Waterleaf family and are sometimes called Scorpian-Weeds because their long, somewhat weak stems often bend over and remind some observers of the arching back of a scorpion. In addition, several of the species have flowers that grow in twisting clusters, not unlike the shape of the arachnid's curling tail.

Some places along the AT you are likely to encounter one of the Phacelias: In Newfound Gap in Great Smoky Mountains National Park, on Big Bald, and north of Overmountain Shelter along the North Carolina–Tennessee border; and on Whitetop Mountain, in Elk Garden, and in the Mount Rogers area in southwest Virginia.

LARGE-FLOWERED TRILLIUM

Trillium grandiflorum

FLOWER:
With the most massive flower of all of the Trilliums, the blossoms of the Large-Flowered Trillium can grow to be four inches wide. The three wavy-edged petals overlap at the base, forming a tube—in which there are six stamens with yellow anthers.

BLOOM SEASON:
April to June

LEAVES AND STEM:
The three- to six-inch-long leaves are nearly stalkless and grow in a whorl of three. The plant may reach up to eighteen inches in height.

RANGE:
Georgia to Maine

When you learn how difficult it is for Trilliums to come to flower, you may wonder how they cover entire hillsides with acres of blooming plants. After pollination, a Trillium flower develops into a berrylike fruit. Eventually, enlarging seeds inside the fruit break open the capsule and fall to the ground. These seeds fall on fertile soil or are carried underground by ants (where nodules attached to the seeds provide a tasty repast). Once underground, the seed spends two years in the soil: The first year it germinates, the second it sends out a shoot. For four or more years, the plant continues to develop leaves. Finally, after a minimum of six years from the time the seed touched the ground, the marvelous three-petaled blossom will appear (and it will continue to do so for many seasons if its environment remains undisturbed).

The Large-Flowered Trillium is probably the most widespread of the Trilliums to be seen along the trail. Those lucky enough to be hiking the trail in northern Virginia in the springtime are in for a spectacular treat: The AT passes through the G. Richard Thompson Wildlife Management Area, which is believed to have the largest colony of Large-Flowered Trilliums in the country—estimated to contain over eighteen million individual plants!

Because its petals turn pink as it ages, the Large-Flowered Trillium can be mistaken for Catesby's Trillium (*Trillium catesbaei*; see page 196), whose blossoms may go through the same change. For a discussion on other Trilliums found in the Appalachian Mountains, see page 36.

Some places along the AT you are likely to encounter one of the Trilliums: Between Max Patch and Hot Springs in North Carolina; north of Angel's Rest in southwest Virginia; Petite's Gap, Thunder Ridge, and The Priest in central Virginia; near the Laurel Prong Trail in Shenandoah National Park; on the side trail to Trico firetower in Maryland; on Wildcat Ridge in New Hampshire; and north of East B Hill Road, and south and north of ME 27 in Maine.

PAINTED TRILLIUM

Trillium undulatum

FLOWER:
The three, white, recurved petals have an inverted pink V at their bases, from which emanate noticeable pink veins. Three green sepals grow in a whorl immediately below the petals.

BLOOM SEASON:
April to June

LEAVES AND STEM:
Growing beneath the flower is a whorl of three ovate, and noticeably stalked, leaves. Tapering to a point, they sometimes turn slightly purple after the plant has flowered.

RANGE:
Most common from Georgia to Pennsylvania/New Jersey, but may be found farther north.

In a season rife with showy blossoms, there is no doubt that the Trilliums are some of springtime's most flamboyant flowers. Of course, they are just following the fashion of other members of the Lily family, a grouping that is well-known for its ostentatiousness. With its splashes of purple and its crinkly edged petals—which give the flower the appearance of an aristocratic linen paper—the Painted Trillium may just be the most outstanding of its genus. (The species name of *undulatum* means "wavy" and refers to the petals' edges.)

All members of the genus *Trillium* (*Tri* is Latin for "trio") have three leaves, flowers with three petals and three sepals, ovaries with three cells, and fruits with three ribs.

Of the other Trilliums you may find along the trail, Purple Trillium (*Trillium erectum;* see page 197) is probably the most common. Also known as Wake-Robin—a name often applied to all Trilliums—it ranges from Georgia into most of New England. Ranging from Georgia to Maryland and Pennsylvania, Toadshade Trillium (*Trillium sessile;* see page 197) also has a purple blossom, but its petals (and sepals) remain erect instead of spreading outward. A more southern plant found in Georgia, North Carolina, and Tennessee, Vasey's Trillium (*Trillium vaseyi;* see page 197) is larger with a usually nodding, purple blossom. See page 34 for a discussion on other AT Trilliums.

Some places along the AT you are likely to encounter one of the Trilliums: Between Max Patch and Hot Springs in North Carolina; at Petite's Gap, Thunder Ridge, and The Priest in central Virginia; near the Laurel Prong Trail in Shenandoah National Park in northeastern Virginia; on the side trail to Trico firetower in Maryland; on Wildcat Ridge in New Hampshire; and north of East B Hill Road, and south and north of ME 27 in Maine.

LILY OF
THE VALLEY

Convallaria majuscula

FLOWER:

The delicate, white, bell-shaped flowers of the Lily of the Valley hang in loose clusters on the side of a five- to ten-inch stem.

BLOOM SEASON:

April to June

LEAVES AND STEM:

Rising above the flowers, the six- to twelve-inch leaves have noticeable veins, are broadly elliptical, and—to some degree—resemble those of the Ramps (Allium tricoccum; see page 76).

RANGE:

Georgia/North Carolina to Virginia

Lily of the Valley is not an extremely rare plant along the southern portion of the AT, but then again, it is so seldom seen that coming across its dangling white flowers is cause enough to pause and enjoy its frail loveliness—and the wonderful fragrance it adds to the forest air.

If you spy one of these plants, it may actually be a close relative. Imported from the Old World to be grown in floral gardens, *Convallaria majalis* looks almost identical to its North American relative, though it tends to form colonies while *Convallaria majuscula* does not. Escaping from the gardens, it has now become naturalized and grows in the same range and environments as *Convallaria majuscula*.

Europeans have long subscribed many medicinal uses to the Lily of the Valley. Around the beginning of the seventeenth century, herbalist John Gerrard wrote, "the floures . . . put into a glasse and set in a hill of ants, close stopped for the space of a moneth, and then taken out, therein you shall finde a liquor that appeaseth the paine and griefe of gout." In his book *Kidnapped*, Robert Louis Stevenson describes this same process to make the liquor and then says, "It is good, ill or well, and whether man or woman. Likewise for sprains, rub it in; and for colic, a great spoonful in the hour." A substance found in Lily of the Valley has been used as a substitute for digitalis, a powerful drug that helps many people survive the complications associated with heart disease.

Old World folklore holds that as Mary wept at the foot of the cross, her tears became Lily of the Valley flowers, thus giving the plant its other common names—Our Lady's Tears and Mary's Tears.

Some places along the AT you are likely to encounter Lily of the Valley: South of Hot Springs in North Carolina; between Dismal Creek and the New River in southwest Virginia; and north of Campbell Shelter, in Black Horse Gap, on Thunder Ridge, and near Jennings Creek in central Virginia.

BOWMAN'S ROOT

Gillenia trifoliata

A long-blooming plant that blooms from late April through July, Bowman's Root can be found inhabiting rich woodlands and the disturbed soils along the sides of roads. Oftentimes it grows so dense, lush, and tall that it almost looks like a shrub. Both the branches and the petals of the flowers are slightly twisted, giving the entire plant a somewhat rough and ragged mien. The noticeably red calyx cup remains after the petals fall off, producing a plant with a slightly different countenance.

Native Americans dried the roots and ground them into a powder to be used as a laxative or an emetic (an agent that enduces vomiting). This may have given rise to the plant's other common name: Indian Physic. The origin of the name Bowman's Root remains a mystery.

A more southern plant that may rarely be seen along the trail, American Ipecac (*Gillenia stipulata* or *Porteranthus stipulatus*) looks very similar to Bowman's Root. But instead of three segments, its leaves appear to have five parts because the stipules (the small appendages at the base of the leaf stalk) are greatly enlarged and appear to be leaflets.

When looking to other sources for further information about Bowman's Root, you should be aware that some reference books follow the classification of John T. Kartesz and list the plant as *Porteranthus trifoliatus*.

Some places along the AT you are likely to encounter Bowman's Root: Side trails around Standing Indian Mountain in North Carolina; and Catawba Mountain in central Virginia.

SMOOTH
SOLOMON'S SEAL

Polygonatum biflorum

FLOWER:

The half-inch, greenish-white, bell-shaped flowers of the Smooth Solomon's Seal droop from the leaf axils in (usually) pairs.

BLOOM SEASON:

May to June

LEAVES AND STEM:

The sessile leaves (meaning they have no stalk) are arranged alternately on the one- to three-foot, arching stem.

RANGE:

Georgia to southern New England

Because these plants cannot tolerate direct sunlight, AT hikers do not encounter the Solomon's Seals until the tree canopy has begun to leaf out. Once they do begin to grow, however, these stately plants are hard to miss, as they often lean over the trail on long, gracefully arching stems.

Of the several species found in the Appalachian Mountains, the Great Solomon's Seal (*Polygonatum canaliculatum*) is the largest, with the longest leaves, the longest stem, and the most numerous flowers. Possibly the most common of the genus found along the trail, Smooth Solomon's Seal is smaller and has fewer flowers (most often a pair) dangling from the leaf axils. Hairy Solomon's Seal (*Polygonatum pubescens*) can be distinguished by hairs that grow on the underside of the leaves along the veins. Similar in appearance to the Solomon's Seals, Twisted Stalk (*Streptopus roseus;* see page 197) has a bent or crooked stem and pink-tinted flowers. See False Solomon's Seal (*Smilacina racemosa;* see page 48) to learn how to differentiate it from the Solomon's Seals.

There is much debate about the derivation of the common name. The most widely accepted story suggests that the scar, which appears when the leaf stalks break off of the underground rootstock at the end of the growing season, resembles King Solomon's official seal. (Incidentally, these scars are produced annually; it is possible to count them to determine the age of an individual plant, some of which have been found to be more than half a century old.)

Some places along the AT you are likely to encounter one of the Solomon's Seals: North of Nibblewill Gap in Georgia; near Spring Mountain Shelter on the North Carolina–Tennessee border; between High Rocks and Spivey Gap in North Carolina; north of Boy Scout Shelter, and along Humpback Mountain in central Virginia; between Hemlock Springs Campsite and Sunk Mine Road in New York; Sages Ravine on the Connecticut–Massachusetts border; and along the Housatonic River in Massachusetts.

SWEET CICELY

Osmorhiza claytoni

FLOWER:

The five-petaled flowers are so small as to be almost indistinguishable. They are noticeable only because they grow in sparse clusters at the top of the plant.

BLOOM SEASON:

May to June

LEAVES AND STEM:

The hairy, one- to three-foot stem has alternate, dull-toothed, fernlike, compound leaves.

RANGE:

Georgia to Maine

Before the days of mass-produced candy and other store-bought confections, the roots of Sweet Cicely, which resemble carrots, were a favorite treat among country people; when chewed, the tubers release a refreshing anise- or licorice-like flavor. It was this trait, in fact, which has given the plant its genus name, *Osmorhiza.* When combined, the Greek words *Osme* and *rhiza* come to mean "scented root." However, it is not just the underground portion of the plant that possesses the enjoyable taste and aroma. When crushed, the leaves yield a pleasing odor, and even the slender, green fruits, which are tapered at both ends and fuzzy along the ribs, are said to have a spicy flavor. All of this has given rise to the plant's common name of Cicely, which is a derivation of the Greek word *seseli*, meaning "sweet-smelling plant."

A relative found ranging from Virginia to Maine, Smooth Sweet Cicely (*Osmorhiza longistylis*) is so similar in appearance that about the only way to distinguish it from Sweet Cicely is that it has a nearly hairless stem. Both species have a tendency to favor moist, rich, deciduous forests, wooded slopes, and stream banks.

Along with Cow Parsnip (*Heracleum lanatum;* see page 82) and Queen Anne's Lace (*Daucus carota;* see page 72), the Sweet Cicelys are members of the Parsley family, of which there are close to three hundred genera and three thousand species. Among the ones familiar to most of us are celery, carrot, parsnip, parsley, caraway, anise, dill, and coriander.

Some places along the AT you are likely to encounter one of the Sweet Cicelys: North of Angel's Rest in southwest Virginia; north of Bryant Ridge Shelter in central Virginia; throughout Shenandoah National Park; and on the east side of Ore Hill, and between Trident Col and Page Pond in New Hampshire.

STARFLOWER

Trientalis borealis

FLOWER:

The two, frail, white flowers of the Starflower have six to seven pointed petals and seven, golden, anther-tipped stamens. Each flower is at the top of a thin and easily broken stalk.

BLOOM SEASON:

May to June

LEAVES AND STEM:

A whorl of seven to nine leaves grows below the pair of flowers. The lance-shaped leaves, pointed on both sides, can vary quite widely in size, growing anywhere from one and a half inches to over four inches long.

RANGE:

Virginia to Maine

Most often found in the cool woods of the higher slopes or in moist thickets beside shady brooks along the AT, Starflower becomes more common the farther north hikers travel from Virginia. In fact, it can be found thriving as far north as Newfoundland, Nova Scotia, and Labrador in Canada; its species name of *borealis* suggests that it is a plant more at home in subalpine regions than in warm, deciduous forests. The genus name, *Trientalis*, comes from a Latin word that roughly translates to mean "one-third of a foot" and refers to the height the plant often attains.

Sometimes called Chickweed Wintergreen, Starflower often grows in large, dense patches, a result of a creeping underground rootstock that sends up erect branches, three to nine inches in height. Starflower also reproduces the more traditional way—from seeds.

Starflowers are members of the Primrose family, which includes Whorled Loosestrife (*Lysimachia quadrifolia;* see page 108), ranging from Georgia to Maine. A more southern member of the family is Shooting-Star (*Dodecatheon meadia*), which can be found in isolated spots from Georgia to Virginia; above its rosette of narrowly elliptic, basal leaves grow a loose cluster of white to pink flowers whose petals point backward in a very distinctive shooting-star shape.

Some places along the AT you are likely to encounter Starflower: Between Floyd Mountain and Parkers Gap in central Virginia; in the forest near White Rocks Cliff in Vermont; between Pinkham Notch and Wildcat Mountain in New Hampshire; and north of East B Hill Road and in the Crocker Mountains in Maine.

FALSE SOLOMON'S SEAL

Smilacina racemosa

FLOWER:
   The False Solomon's Seal has dozens of tiny, off-white flowers which form a triangular-shaped terminal cluster.

BLOOM SEASON:
   May to July

LEAVES AND STEM:
   Ranging from one to three feet in length, the stem makes a bit of a bend at the point where each of the elliptical, three- to six-inch leaves grow alternately upon it. The heavily veined leaves are hairy underneath.

RANGE:
   Georgia to Maine

Since they emerge at the same time and share similar appearances, it can sometimes be difficult to distinguish the False Solomon's Seals from the Solomon's Seals (genus *Polygonatum;* see page 42). It is best done at either the flowering or fruit-bearing time. The Solomon's Seals' little bell-shaped flowers hang down from the leaf axils along the stem, while the tiny, starred blossoms of the False Solomon's Seals extend from the end of the stem. Later in the year, the Solomon's Seals' fruit is a dark blue (almost black) berry, easily differentiated from the red berries of the False Solomon's Seals.

Because the blossoms are so small (no more than one-eighth-inch wide), it is easy to overlook the subtle beauty of the False Solomon's Seal's flowers. Six stamens rise from the center of the three petals and three petal-like sepals, which, when covered with dew and highlighted by a rising sun, can look like sparkling snowflakes. Later in the year, the False Solomon's Seal's bright red berries and chartreuse-gold leaves add a welcome dash of color to the forest floor.

Found ranging from Virginia/West Virginia to New England, Star-Flowered False Solomon's Seal (*Smilacina stellata*) has a shorter stem than the False Solomon's Seal, its star-shaped flowers are larger and its leaves clasp the stem.

When looking to other sources for further information about the False Solomon's Seals, you should be aware that some books follow the classifications of John T. Kartesz and place them within the genus *Maianthemum*.

Some places along the AT you are likely to encounter one of the False Solomon's Seals: On Little Bald on the North Carolina–Tennessee border; north of Boy Scout Shelter, in Petites Gap, and along Humpback Mountain in central Virginia; between Hemlock Springs Campsite and Sunk Mine Road in New York; between MA 2 and Seth Warner Shelter in Massachusetts and Vermont; and North Crocker Mountain in Maine.

49

LABRADOR TEA

Ledum groenlandicum

FLOWER:
The white, one-half-inch-wide flowers of the Labrador Tea have five petals and grow in tight, round, terminal clusters.

BLOOM SEASON:
May to July

LEAVES AND STEM:
The one-half- to three-inch, leathery, evergreen leaves of this low-growing bush grow on short stalks, are rolled along their edges, and are narrowly oblong.

RANGE:
Almost exclusively in northern New England

The hairy twigs and rusty-brown wool on the underside of the plant's leaves make it quite easy to recognize Labrador Tea while hiking along the AT. Be on the lookout for it as you pass through a black spruce or white spruce forest or while traversing the boggy, higher elevations of northern New England. Native Americans and early settlers brewed a refreshing tea from the leaves, and folk medicine says that a syrup made from the tea is useful in treating coughs. Researchers have found the tea to be rich in Vitamin C, and there is currently a thriving mail-order business that annually ships hundreds of pounds of the leaves to enthusiasts throughout Canada and the United States. Humans are not the only ones to enjoy the plant; its twigs and leaves are a favorite browse of moose.

Labrador Tea is a member of the Heath family, and like some of its relatives, such as the Mountain Laurel (*Kalmia latifolia;* see page 146), its fruit develops into a capsule containing hundreds of seeds which, individually, are no larger than a speck of dust.

This plant can be an important link in helping to restore the health of a forest or a bog after a fire. Because its rootstocks grow deeply into the ground—up to twenty inches below the surface in some cases—it can survive the ravages of heat. New shoots rising from the rootstock will be some of the first to emerge and begin the process of revegetation after a fire.

Some places along the AT you are likely to encounter Labrador Tea: Throughout the White Mountains, especially on Kinsman Ridge and between Mount Pierce and Lakes of the Clouds Hut in New Hampshire; north of the New Hampshire-Maine border; and in the alpine zones of Saddleback, The Horn, and Saddleback Jr. in Maine.

GALAX

Galax aphylla

It is next to impossible to take a full day's hike along the AT between Georgia and Virginia and not come across some Galax. The plant forms dense carpets beside the pathway and upon the forest floor, covering extensive areas of the mountains with its evergreen leaves. Early in the season the leaves are almost a yellowish green, but they turn to a rich and shiny deep green by the middle of summer. During the cooler fall and winter months the leaves offer a bit of welcome color as they transform themselves into a bronze or dull crimson hue.

When picked, the leaves remain green a long time, a trait that led in the past to overharvesting of the plant. A wildflower guide published around the turn of the twentieth century states that the mountain people picked Galax plants by the millions and shipped them to commercial florists throughout the country. Sadly, even recently, people have been caught harvesting the plant from national forests and national parklands—where picking any flower is illegal.

Even when not in bloom, Galax has a peculiar smell, and many hikers become aware of the plant long before seeing it. Some people say it has a sweet, but pungent, aroma. Others insist the odor is more akin to a decaying body.

When looking to different sources for further information about Galax, you should be aware that some books follow the classifications of John T. Kartesz and list it as *Galax urceolata*. In addition, the fact that some references refer to the plant as *Galax rotundifolia* indicate that it has undergone a name change under Gray's classification system.

Some places along the AT you are likely to encounter Galax: At Indian Grave Gap and on Tray Mountain in Georgia; above the Nantahala River, between Cheoah Bald and Stecoah Gap, and between High Rocks and Spivey Gap in North Carolina; and at Black Horse Gap, near Matts Creek, and between Floyd Mountain and Parkers Gap Road in central Virginia.

PARTRIDGEBERRY

Mitchella repens

FLOWER:
These small, white to pinkish flowers grow in pairs that join at their bases to the end of a creeping stem.

BLOOM SEASON:
May to July

LEAVES AND STEM:
The small, one-half- to three-quarter-inch evergreen leaves are smooth, shiny, and opposite on long, trailing stems that grow close to the ground.

RANGE:
Georgia to Maine

The Partridgeberry is such an interesting plant that it warrants getting down on hands and knees to observe. Two white flowers, blooming in early summer, fuse together to produce one tiny berry. A close examination of that berry, which changes from green to red during the cooler months, will reveal two scars—one from each flower.

The flowers themselves deserve careful observation, too. They may grow in pairs, but each is different from the other. One has a long pistil and a short stamen while the other is just the opposite—a short pistil and a long stamen. This dimorphism helps to ensure cross-pollination by insects and prevents the flowers from self-fertilizing. Incidentally, both flowers of the pair must be fertilized for the fruit to develop.

The genus name of *Mitchella* honors John Mitchell, who saved countless lives during the Philadelphia yellow fever epidemic of the 1700s by developing a way to treat victims stricken with the disease. The species name of *repens* indicates that the plant creeps or trails along the ground. (For this same reason, Trailing Arbutus was given the scientific name of *Epigaea repens*; see page 12) Partridgeberry's common name refers to the fact that wild partridges (and wild turkeys and quail) feed upon the fruit.

The plant provides important ground cover to the forest floor; its roots are shallow, but they intertwine so completely that they form a compact mat, which helps stabilize the soil and keeps it from washing away.

Some places along the AT you are likely to encounter Partridgeberry: Near Gooch Gap Shelter in Georgia; Fork Mountain and James River Face Wilderness in central Virginia; Mount Greylock in Massachusetts; between MA 2 and Seth Warner Shelter in Massachusetts and Vermont; and beside the Saco River in New Hampshire.

WHITE CLINTONIA

Clintonia umbellulata

FLOWER:
The one-half-inch flowers, which grow in an umbel at the top of a thin, eight- to twenty-inch stalk, have three white petals and three white petal-like sepals which are usually dotted with green and purple.

BLOOM SEASON:
May to July

LEAVES AND STEM:
The oval-shaped, hairy leaves grow in a basal whorl.

RANGE:
Georgia to New Jersey/New York

Much like the relative that it resembles—the Bluebead Lily (*Clintonia borealis;* see page 106)—the most striking thing about the White Clintonia is not its flowers, but its leaves. Each plant has two to five, richly green, basal leaves that are broadly oval-shaped, have tiny hairs along their margins and midribs, and can reach ten inches or more in length. Young leaves have been boiled and used as a substitute for collards or other greens.

Sometime in midsummer the petals of the flowers fall off and are replaced by small clusters of shiny dark blue (almost black) berries, which Native Americans used to produce a rich-colored dye.

The plant's common and genus names honor Dewitt Clinton, a governor of New York, a noted author of several natural history books, and the main proponent for the construction of the Erie Canal. Also called Speckled Wood Lily, White Clintonia grows best in rich, moist forests. It becomes increasingly less common the further north a hiker travels from the southern states.

Some other members of the Lily family you may happen to discover inhabiting AT lands include Fly Poison (*Amianthium muscaetoxicum;* see page 60); Dogtooth Violet (*Erythronium americanum;* see page 94); Canada Mayflower (*Maianthemum canadense;* see page 58); Wild Oats (*Uvularia sessilifolia;* see page 102); and False Hellebore (*Veratrum viride;* see page 194).

Some places along the AT you are likely to encounter White Clintonia: Around Thunder Hill in central Virginia; in Compton Gap in Shenandoah National Park; and just north of the Bear Mountain summit in Connecticut.

CANADA MAYFLOWER

Maianthemum canadense

The rootstocks of the Canada Mayflower creep so extensively and send up so many shoots that it is rare to come across the plant where it has not formed a large colony carpeting a sizable area of the forest floor. The flowers are quite fragrant, so you may smell the colony before you see them.

Once the calendar comes into the heat of August afternoons, the blossoms are replaced by tightly packed clusters of berries. When they first appear, these fruits are pale green with spots, but they turn a mottled dull red as the cooler nights of autumn arrive. Trying to build up body fat in preparation for the harshness of the coming winter, grouse, chipmunks, and other rodents forage on these berries for extended periods of time.

With its zigzagging stem and cluster of white flowers, Canada Mayflower may sometimes be mistaken for one of the False Solomon's Seals (genus *Smilacina;* see page 48). However, the Canada Mayflower is usually much shorter and will only have two to three leaves (instead of many) along the length of its stem.

Also called Wild or False Lily of the Valley, Canada Mayflower receives its genus name of *Maianthemum* from Greek mythology. The goddess Maia—the mother of Hermes—was said to be so beautiful that only a plant as lovely as this one could be named in her honor. As is often the case, another source disagrees with this story and suggests *Maianthemum* merely stands for May, the month in which the flower blooms.

Some places along the AT you are likely to encounter Canada Mayflower: Between High Rocks and Spivey Gap in North Carolina; between Floyd Mountain and Parkers Gap Road in central Virginia; within the Mount Greylock State Reservation in Massachusetts; on Killington Peak and Mosley Hill in Vermont; between Lowe's Bald Spot and Pinkham Notch, and in Trident Col in New Hampshire; and north and south of the Sandy River in Maine.

FLY POISON

*Amianthium
muscaetoxicum*

FLOWER:
Growing in compact, cylindrical clusters on the top of the stem, the one-half-inch-wide flowers have three petals and three petal-like sepals. Starting out white, the blossoms become greenish or purplish as they age (they remain on the plant while the fruit is ripening).

BLOOM SEASON:
May to July

LEAVES AND STEM:
The basal leaves are very grass-like in appearance, are about three-quarters of an inch wide, and may reach lengths of more than twelve inches. Leaves that happen to occur along the length of the one- to four-foot stem are much smaller and hardly noticeable.

RANGE:
Georgia to Pennsylvania

If you have ever had the pleasure of walking through a field of Bear Grass (*Xerophyllum tenax*) in the northern Rocky Mountains, you will be excited to see Fly Poison scattered about in the woodlands along the AT. While it does not grow quite as tall as its western relative in the Lily family, the Fly Poison's cluster of white flowers at the top of its stem can be almost as large and as impressive.

As its name implies, all parts of this plant (especially the rootstock) contain toxic alkaloids, and it has been known to be fatal to grazing livestock. Consumption by humans may lead to vomiting, dizziness, heart problems, and death. The toxin is so strong that some sources caution you to refrain from even touching the plant and advise washing your hands immediately if you do so.

Before the days of commercially produced insecticides, early American settlers mixed the crushed root bulb with sugar to attract and kill flies. The species name reflects this practice; *muscae* is Latin for "flies" and *toxicum* translates as "poison."

Often found growing in the same areas as Fly Poison, Turkeybeard (*Xerophyllum asphodeloides*) has the same general appearance, but its flower clusters tend to be more rounded, and its basal leaves are much, much narrower.

When looking to other sources for further information about Fly Poison, you should be aware that some books follow the classifications of John T. Kartesz and list it as *Amianthium muscitoxicum*.

Some places along the AT you are likely to encounter Fly Poison or Turkeybeard: At Camp Creek Bald on the North Carolina–Tennessee border; on Tinker Mountain, the south side of Fork Mountain, Thunder Hill, and Bald Knob in central Virginia; and throughout Shenandoah National Park.

GOLDTHREAD

Coptis groenlandica

FLOWER:

What appear to be the petals on Goldthread are actually five to seven white sepals. The one-half-inch-in-diameter flowers are solitary on leafless stalks.

BLOOM SEASON:

May to July

LEAVES AND STEM:

The basal, evergreen leaves are divided into three rounded leaflets that are deeply toothed.

RANGE:

Georgia/North Carolina to Maine

Goldthread receives its common name from the tiny, bright yellow, thread-thin rootstocks that grow just below the surface of the ground. This is one of the most far-ranging wildflowers found along the AT, for in addition to inhabiting the higher elevations from Georgia/North Carolina to Maine, the plant can be found as far north as the Arctic Circle of Canada and Alaska.

Preferring swamps, bogs, coniferous forests, and the disturbed soil along road banks and trails, Goldthread has adapted well to the cooler, harsher environments in which it grows. Its leathery, evergreen leaves and hardy stems help prevent desiccation and damage from ice storms and high winds, while the shallow-growing rootstocks enable it to be one of the first plants to take advantage of any moisture which seeps below the surface. In addition, the plant is not just dependent on cross-fertilization to produce seeds, but is also able to send up new shoots from its roots. This is why you will often see Goldthread growing in large colonies spreading across the forest floor. The intertwining network of roots in these colonies make the plant an important ground cover, helping to hold the soil together and prevent erosion.

It almost takes a magnifying glass to find the petals of the flower which grow in the center of the surrounding white sepals. These obscure, club-shaped petals are the reason that insects visit the plant—the petals contain the nectar.

Native Americans and early settlers chewed Goldthread roots to treat mouth sores and made a tea from the plant to be used as an eyewash.

Some places along the AT you are likely to encounter Goldthread: Throughout the Presidential Mountains, and between Pinkham Notch and Crawford Notch in New Hampshire; and on Wyman Mountain, south of Saddleback, and near Bigelow Mountain in Maine.

BUNCHBERRY

Cornus canadensis

FLOWER:

*What looks like petals are actu-
ally four, large, white, leaf bracts,
which surround the small cluster of
tiny, yellowish green flowers.*

BLOOM SEASON:

May to July

LEAVES AND STEM:

*Resembling those of the Dogwood
trees, the one-and-a-half- to three-
inch-long leaves grow in a whorl
under the leaf bracts and flowers.
Each pointed, ovate leaf has very
noticeable veins.*

RANGE:

*Although it chiefly occurs in the
northern New England States,
Bunchberry is sometimes found as
far south as Shenandoah National
Park—but rarely on AT lands.*

Bunchberry has the distinction of being one of only two species in the Dogwood family to be an herb rather than a shrub or a tree. The other species, Northern Dwarf Cornel (*Cornus suecica*), grows in southern Canada.

Often found in the same environments as Partridgeberry (*Mitchella repens;* see page 54) and Goldthread (*Coptis groenlandica;* see page 62), the Bunchberry reproduces from clones that rise from its woody rhizomes, as well as propagating itself through seeds. Thus, you will often find the plant growing in large colonies spreading out for dozens of feet in all directions.

Looking like a miniature copy of its larger relatives, the Dogwood trees, Bunchberry is a thing of beauty at any time of the year. From May to July the whorl of green leaves below the pure-white leaf bracts calls to mind Christmas ornaments or corsages strewn across the ground. In late summer the plant produces clusters of bright scarlet berries (hence its common name) that not only brighten up the dreariest of damp and foggy days, but are also edible. Although a bit tart when eaten raw, they make a great pudding when cooked with sugar and lemon. Vireos, veeries, and other woodland birds also seem to enjoy the fruits. In the fall and into early winter, the leaves are a rich crimson hue, decorating an otherwise brown and gray forest floor.

Some places along the AT you are likely to encounter Bunchberry: Between Race Mountain and Mount Everett in Massachusetts; along Glastenbury Mountain, near White Rocks Cliff, and on the slopes of Killington Peak in Vermont; between Mount Jackson and Mizpah Spring Hut in New Hampshire; south of Saddleback, in the Crocker Mountains, and on the south side of Moxie Bald Mountain in Maine.

COMMON WOOD SORRELL

Oxalis montana

FLOWER:

Somewhat resembling those of the Spring Beauty (Claytonia virginica; see page 128), *the flowers of the Wood Sorrel have five, white—sometimes pale pink—petals that are marked with very noticeable dark pink to purple veins and are usually notched at the tips.*

BLOOM SEASON:

May to July

LEAVES AND STEM:

The basal leaves are divided into three heart-shaped segments that join together to form a shamrock or clover shape.

RANGE:

Georgia/North Carolina to Maine

There are some places along the trail—especially in the moist, evergreen forests of New England—that the shamrock-shaped leaves of the Common Wood Sorrel are so rich and plentiful, you almost expect to turn a corner and spy a leprechaun leaning against a moss-covered rock.

The plant, in fact, has a strong relationship with Ireland. Legend says St. Patrick used the Wood Sorrel and not the Shamrock to explain the Christian Doctrine of the Trinity (the belief that three separate entities of God exist as one). Laura C. Martin, in her book *Wildflower Folklore*, says that before the Irish were converted to Christianity, the Wood Sorrel leaf was used as a symbol by the Druids and had a place in the Celtic sun wheel.

The plant's genus name comes from the Greek and roughly translates as "sharply acid." The stalks and leaves do have an acidic, lemonlike taste and can be a refreshing treat when chewed or added to a fresh salad. Native Americans made a drink from the leaves that was said to taste a bit like lemonade. Although the Native Americans did not know the plants contained a high concentration of vitamin C, they ate large amounts of it raw because they knew it helped to prevent "winter sickness" (known to us today as scurvy).

When looking to other sources for further information about the Common Wood Sorrel, you should be aware that its name within Gray's classification system has changed, and that some books refer to it as *Oxalis acetosella*.

Some places along the AT you are likely to encounter Wood Sorrel: On Fork Mountain in central Virginia; in October Mountain State Forest, and between Mount Greylock and Mount Fitch in Massachusetts; along Glastenbury Mountain, near White Rocks Cliff, and on the slopes of Killington Peak in Vermont; between Mount Webster and Mizpah Spring Hut, and in Pinkhan Notch in New Hampshire; and on Wyman Mountain and the Crocker Mountains in Maine.

GINSENG

Panax quinquefolius

The white to pale yellow-green flowers (of about one-tenth inch in size) grow in small, rounded clusters from the axil of the three leaves.

May to August

At the end of an eight- to twenty-inch stem, the three leaves are divided into five, pointed, toothed leaflets.

Georgia to Maine

Although it has a range that takes in all the states of the AT, Ginseng is most often thought of as a Southern and Cove Hardwood Forest inhabitant. Southerners have long looked upon the plant as a source of income, yet it is not gathered for its flowers and foliage, but rather its roots. Many Chinese have faith in the Doctrine of Signatures—the belief that a plant can cure the ailing body part it resembles. (For example, it is believed that members of the Snapdragon family are useful in treating throat sicknesses because of the mouth-and-throat form of the blossoms.) The forked roots of the Ginseng resemble the trunk and legs of a man (ginseng is taken from the Chinese *Jin-chen*, which means "manlike" or "trouser-shaped"). For this reason, the roots have been revered in China for hundreds of years as an overall health remedy and an aphrodisiac. Even in the United States there is ongoing research into the medicinal value of Ginseng and a few preliminary reports say it is of some aid to the endocrine glands which help regulate the flow of hormones; the greatest benefits seem to be to the aged and those under stress.

Ginseng has been gathered so extensively through the years that it has become increasingly harder to find. Now under strict guidelines, the roots are still harvested and offered to the buyers who travel the southern mountains, visiting the many temporary markets set up during the fall. In Georgia alone it is estimated that the plant brings in more than three million dollars each year.

(Complying with the request of several botanical authorities, we have elected not to include any specific locations for Ginseng because it is a collected and harvested plant that is considered to be threatened in a couple of states and is on the way to being declared rare or endangered in several others.)

MOUNTAIN SANDWORT

Arenaria groenlandica

FLOWER:

The half-inch-wide white flowers of the Mountain Sandwort are slightly translucent and have five separate petals which have small notches on them. The blossoms usually grow on the tip of the very slender stems, but are often seen extending below the middle of the stem.

BLOOM SEASON:

May to September

LEAVES AND STEM:

The leaves are only one-half-inch long and are so narrow that they almost resemble evergreen needles. Most often these basal leaves form mats from which the flower stems rise.

RANGE:

The plant and its variant species cling to the higher elevations from Georgia to New York; they are a bit more common along the rocky ridgelines and summits of New England.

As evidenced by its species name of *groenlandica*, the Mountain Sandwort is a plant that is more at home in the arctic regions of Greenland and Canada than it is in the mountains of the AT. It is most often found along the trail growing in the loose, sandy soil of cracks and crevices of large slabs of granite or along the edges of sandstone pavements. Its habitat is reflected in its genus name of *Arenaria*, which is Latin for "sand."

Like most plants of the tundra, Mountain Sandwort is low-growing (no more than five inches in height), so as to expose itself as little as possible to the harsh conditions of its environment, such as ice storms and near-constant cold winds.

There are a number of variant species of the Mountain Sandwort that may possibly be found along the AT, but it is sometimes hard to make an exact identification. In addition, some species crossbreed and hybridize. *Arenaria groenlandica* variety *glabra* has stems that may be either simple or forked, but it rarely forms mats. *Minuartia groenlandica* is considered a rare plant in Virginia. It does form mats, and about the only difference between it and *Arenaria groenlandica* is that its petals and sepals are slightly larger (about one millimeter).

When looking to other sources for further information about the Mountain Sandworts, you should be aware that some reference books list their genus name as *Sabulina*.

Some places along the AT you are likely to encounter Mountain Sandwort: Less than one mile north of Boy Scout Shelter in central Virginia; on Mount Jackson in New Hampshire; and on Old Speck Mountain, Baldpate Mountain, Bigelow Mountain, and above the treeline on Saddleback and in the col south of The Horn in Maine.

QUEEN ANNE'S
LACE
Daucus carota

The individual flowers are so small as to be indistinguishable, but they do grow in a flat-topped cluster three to five inches wide. There is usually a dark red floret in the center of the cluster.

BLOOM SEASON:
May to October

LEAVES AND STEM:
The leaves, growing upon a hairy stem one to four feet high, are pinnately divided and dissected, giving them a fernlike look.

RANGE:
Georgia to Maine

For such a common flower, controversy appears to whirl around Queen Anne's Lace much like the dozens of wasps, bees, and flies attracted to its large umbel of small flowers.

First, there is the matter of the common name. Most authorities attribute it to Queen Anne, England's ruler from 1702 to 1714. According to the standard story, she was fond of fancy lace on her dresses and used the plant as a model. One day, while sewing some lace, she pricked her finger; the one dark red floret in the middle of the flower's umbel is where the drop of blood landed. Another reference book states instead that the plant honors Anne of Denmark, the wife of James I, also an admirer of fine lace.

This plant's other common name, Wild Carrot, points to another controversy—whether it is the progenitor of the cultivated carrot. Many sources, including the well-respected *National Audubon Society Field Guide to North American Flowers*, simply state that the plant was the ancestor of the garden carrot. This theory is strengthened by the fact that the scientific name of the carrot we eat is *Dauscus carota sativa*, implying that it is a subspecies. But upon further investigation, you will find a study which disputes this. Allowing a garden carrot to go uncultivated for several generations, one investigator found that it reverted to a plant "quite distinct from *Daucus carota*." Yet, by going in the other direction, another investigation, in the space of three years, obtained from the roots of the Queen Anne's Lace "roots as fleshy and as large as those of the garden carrot."

Some places along the AT you are likely to encounter Queen Anne's Lace: Between Beech Gap and Big Spring Shelter, and on Max Patch in North Carolina; south of Street Gap along the North Carolina–Tennessee border; on Peters Mountain and on the side trail to Sunset Field in central Virginia; between Mount Algo and CT 341 in Connecticut; and in the fields along MA 41 at South Egremont in Massachusetts.

DIAPENSIA

Diapensia lapponica

FLOWER:
The five lobes of the white flower, growing on a very short stalk, connect to the five stamens.

BLOOM SEASON:
June to July

LEAVES AND STEM:
The leaves and stems of this evergreen plant creep along the ground, creating small tufts.

RANGE:
Northern New England states

Diapensia is one of the few truly alpine flowers to occur along the AT, found almost exclusively above the treeline in the White Mountains of New Hampshire and along the open crests of the higher summits in Maine. Like many plants that exist in such a harsh environment, it grows low to the ground. By forming mats of dense mosslike leaves, it can better withstand the high winds, ice storms, and low temperatures than if it grew as a solitary flower.

Sadly, *Diapensia lapponica* may not exist much longer in the United States if the predictions of global warming prove correct. The plant is pushing the very southern limits of its range, and it would only take a rise in temperature of a couple of degrees to wipe it out. Of course, global warming could bring about many other changes to the natural world as we know it. The great evergreen forests of Vermont, New Hampshire, and Maine would be overtaken by the deciduous forests now found farther south, while the lofty trees inhabiting the mountains to the south of New England would probably be replaced by low-growing vegetation and open meadowlands not unlike the savannas of South America.

There are six genera and close to ten species of the Diapensia family that are native to North America, but there are only two other members of the family that may be found along the AT—and both are southern plants. Growing in great abundance, Galax (*Galax aphylla*; see page 52) ranges from Georgia to Virginia, while Oconee Bells (*Shortia galacifolia*) is a very rare plant found only in the mountains of Georgia and North and South Carolina.

Some places along the AT you are likely to encounter Diapensia: Near the summits of Mount Pierce, Mount Lafayette, and Mount Washington in New Hampshire; and on Mount Carlo, Saddleback, The Horn, Saddleback Jr., and Bigelow Mountain in Maine.

RAMPS

Allium tricoccum

Growing beneath the canopies of Southern and Cove Hardwood Forests is a plant that has played an important role in the lives of Southern Appalachian inhabitants. It was not that long ago that preserving vegetables by canning or freezing was unknown; by the time winter was ending, people were craving fresh green foods. To the rescue came Ramps, which appear in early spring—usually as a pair of lilylike leaves growing in the rich cove soils often beside creeks and small streams.

Sometimes referred to as a Wild Leek, the underground portion of a Ramp is a small onion containing allyl sulphate, the ingredient that gives garlic its taste. Gathered when they are young, these plants are cooked as a vegetable, served in salads, added to soups, used as a seasoning, and, most popularly, fried and mixed with ham and/or eggs. The strong-tasting Ramps have a loyal following unto this day, with Ramp festivals held annually—such as the one near Whitetop Mountain on the AT in southwest Virginia. These festivals have become so popular throughout the plant's range that huge quantities are now harvested to meet the demand. Some botanists are beginning to worry that the Ramp may need to be a protected species sometime in the future.

If permitted to grow, the Ramp's leaves eventually wither away and a cluster of twenty to fifty white flowers bloom on top of a single stem.

Native Americans used the juice of the plant's bulb to treat insect bites and to relieve the aches and pains of a cold.

Some places along the AT you are likely to encounter Ramps: At Beech Gap, near Big Spring Shelter, and between Big Bald and Bald Mountain Shelter in North Carolina; south of Elk Garden, and between I-81 and Davis Path Shelter in southwest Virginia; and along the access trail to Kay Wood Shelter in Massachusetts.

MOUNTAIN SAXIFRAGE

Saxifraga michauxii

FLOWER:
Rising on a hairy stalk six to twenty inches in height, the flowers have five petals. The three large petals are heart-shaped at their base and have a pair of yellow spots, while the two smaller ones have tapering bases and no spots.

BLOOM SEASON:
June to August

LEAVES AND STEM:
The coarsely toothed, three- to seven-inch-long leaves grow in a rosette around the base of the floral stalk.

RANGE:
Georgia to Virginia

Usually found in rocky places along the trail, Mountain Saxifrage receives its name from its ability to grow in such places. People once believed the plants caused the cracks and tiny fissures in which they're rooted—thus the Latin word for "stone," *saxum*, was combined with *fragere*, which means "to break." Because of this belief (and the fact that a European species of Saxifrage has stonelike granules on its roots), herb doctors followed the Doctrine of Signatures in prescribing the plant as a treatment for kidney stones and gallstones.

The species name of *michauxii* honors André Michaux, a French botanist who explored the southern Appalachians extensively in the late 1700s. Collecting flowers, trees, shrubs, and other plants for the French government, it is estimated he shipped back more than 2,500 specimens to be included in the royal gardens.

A relative of Mountain Saxifrage, the Star-Like Saxifrage's (*Saxifraga stellaris*) green basal leaves are thin, and its white flowers appear only on the largest of the plants. Interestingly, it only grows in the United States on Mount Katahdin in Maine. Also found on the slopes of Mount Katahdin—and in the mountains of Vermont and New York—is White Mountain Saxifrage (*Saxifraga aizoon*), which has toothed and tufted basal leaves. Ranging from Georgia to Maine, Early Saxifrage (*Saxifraga virginiensis*) has a floral stalk that is shorter and thicker, and its flower petals lack the small yellow dots.

Some places along the AT you are likely to encounter one of the Saxifrages: Near Jennings Creek and The Priest in central Virginia; between Big Meadows and Skyland in Shenandoah National Park; around St. Johns Ledges in Connecticut; on Mount Greylock in Massachusetts; on Moose Mountain and Holts Ledge in New Hampshire; and in Dunn Notch in Maine.

OXEYE DAISY

*Chrysanthemum
leucanthemum*

FLOWER:
   The inner, yellow, flattened or
depressed, disc flowers are surrounded
by fifteen to thirty-five, outer, white,
ray petals.

BLOOM SEASON:
   June to August

LEAVES AND STEM:
   The narrow, sessile, dark green
leaves are toothed or lobed and
arranged alternately on a stem that
rises one to three feet from the
ground.

RANGE:
   Georgia to Maine

The Oxeye Daisy did not exist in North America until the early settlers began arriving from Europe. Its seeds were probably imported when they were inadvertently included in shipments of crop seeds or in the fodder used to feed livestock on the long ocean voyages from the Old World. Once here, it did not take the plant long to spread across the land, often overtaking open fields and garden lands. It is now found throughout most of the United States and Canada.

The Oxeye Daisy is a member of the Composite family, which Roger Tory Peterson believes to be the most recent one to make its appearance on earth. Despite its late development, it is now the largest of all of the families of flowering plants. The Oxeye Daisy is typical of most of its members, having rays of petals (Peterson refers to them as "strap-shaped flowers") surrounding a center disk of small, tubular flowers. The rays are actually sterile flowers whose main purpose appears to be to serve as a landing pad and an attractant to the insects that will visit and pollinate the fertile, yellow, disc flowers.

By the way, the Daisy almost always has an odd number of petals, so to get the desired result, be sure to start with the right phrase when you use the plant to find out if "she loves me, she loves me not."

When looking to other sources for further information about Oxeye Daisy, you should be aware that some reference books follow the classifications of John T. Kartesz and list it as *Leucanthemum vulgare*.

Some places along the AT you are likely to encounter Oxeye Daisy: South of Street Gap along the North Carolina–Tennessee border; between US 460 and Sinking Creek Valley, and on the side trail to Sunset Field in central Virginia; and in the fields along MA 41 at South Egremont in Massachusetts.

COW PARSNIP

Heracleum lanatum

Growing along streambanks and roadsides, in open meadows, neglected fields and wastelands, and upon the moist ground often found in higher elevations, Cow Parsnip is one of the largest of the wildflower plants to be found along the AT. Not only does it sometimes attain a height of nine to ten feet, it is not unusual for its flower umbels to be close to twelve inches in diameter.

A relative of Queen Anne's Lace (*Daucus carota;* see page 72), of which it bears a bit of a resemblance, Cow Parsnip has been used for centuries as both food and medicine. When spring arrived and the plant world began to awaken from winter's dormancy, Native Americans and early colonists cooked the Cow Parsnip's tender young leaves and stalks and used them as a substitute for fresh garden greens. A tea made from the flowers was used to treat headaches, while a powder made from the dried root was added to bathwater as a treatment for paralysis. The rootstock has also been eaten to treat indigestion and gas pains—yet, cattle eating the root have died! According to recent tests, the substance psoralen, which is found in the root, shows promise in helping those who suffer from psoriasis, leukemia, or AIDS.

Also found ranging throughout all of the AT states, the flowers of the Poison Hemlock (*Conium maculatum*) and the Water Hemlock (*Cicuta maculata*) resemble those of the Cow Parsnip—yet both plants are highly toxic and should be avoided. Poison Hemlock was the plant used to kill Socrates.

When looking to other sources for further information about Cow Parsnip, you should be aware that some reference books classify it as *Heracleum maximum*.

Some places along the AT you are likely to encounter Cow Parsnip: Many of the trail crossings of Skyline Drive in Shenandoah National Park; in the Cumberland Valley of Pennsylvania; near Stony Brook in Connecticut; and between Thistle Hill and the White River in Vermont.

WILD SARSAPARILLA

Aralia nudicaulis

FLOWER:

The tiny white flowers have five noticeably green stamens and grow in round clusters of about two inches in diameter.

BLOOM SEASON:

June to August

LEAVES AND STEM:

The eight- to fifteen-inch-long leaf rises on a single stem and has three branching parts that are divided into three to five toothed leaflets.

RANGE:

Georgia to Maine

Because it reproduces by seeds and by shoots rising up from its creeping rhizomes, Wild Sarsaparilla is most often encountered growing in large colonies. The fragrant rootstock has been used as a substitute for true Sarsaparilla in the making of tea and root beer.

Once the plant stops blooming in late summer, the flowers give way to a cluster of purplish-black berries, which are a favorite food of black bears. In a wonderful example of the web of life—how all things are interrelated and dependent upon each other for survival—studies have shown that Sarsaparilla seeds eaten by bears and then excreted are two to three times more likely to germinate than those seeds not eaten.

Sharing the same range and favoring the same open woods environment as Wild Sarsaparilla, you might also encounter Bristly Sarsaparilla (*Aralia hispida*) while hiking along the AT. A larger plant that may reach four feet in height, its stem is somewhat woody and hairy near the base. In some ways, the Sarsaparillas resemble their relative Ginseng (*Panax quinquefolius;* see page 68), but their flowers grow in three to five clusters on the end of the stalk, whereas Ginseng has only a solitary cluster. In addition, the Sarsaparilla flower clusters are on a stalk that is separate from that of the leaves, while the clusters of Ginseng flowers grow from the leaf stem.

Some places along the AT you are likely to encounter one of the Sarsaparillas: Between High Rocks and Spivey Gap in Tennessee; on Humpback Mountain in central Virginia; between Race Mountain and Mount Everett in Massachusetts; between Prospect Rock and Spruce Peak Shelter in Vermont; between Lowe's Bald Spot and Pinkham Notch in New Hampshire; and the north side of Poplar Ridge in Maine.

DOWNY RATTLESNAKE PLANTAIN

Goodyera pubescens

Growing in a dense cluster at the end of a six- to eighteen-inch hairy spike, the flowers of the Rattlesnake Plantain are so small (about one-quarter inch in diameter) that you will need to get close to study them. Each tiny blossom has two petals and an upper sepal which cover a lower lip.

Late June to August

Appearing in a basal rosette, the broad leaves are bluish green and marked by a network of white veins.

Georgia to Maine

More than its flowers, the most striking thing about the Rattlesnake Plantain is its leaves. Remaining green throughout the year, the mottled leaves are said to resemble the markings on the skin of a rattlesnake—hence the common name. (In addition—if you use your imagination—the flowered spike reminds some people of the rattlesnake's tail.) Following the Doctrine of Signatures, the plants—which are common in both moist and dry woodlands—were often used to treat snake bites. Since there appears to be no special agent in the Rattlesnake Plantain to act as a remedy, it must be assumed most victims recovered only because their bodies were able to fight off the poison.

The genus name of *Goodyera* honors a botanist from the 1600s, John Goodyer. The species name of *pubescens* is Latin for "hairy" and refers to the fine hairs found along the floral spike.

Another Rattlesnake Plantain which inhabits the states through which the AT passes is the Dwarf Rattlesnake Plantain (*Goodyera repens*). A shorter plant that rarely reaches more than ten inches in height, its blossoms are smaller and only grow on one side of the floral spike. This native of boreal and arctic Europe and North America will usually be found in the higher elevations. Checkered Rattlesnake Plantain (*Goodyera tesselata*) only occurs in the most northern New England states and is quite uncommon on the trail. This plant's leaves are more of a dull gray-green with pale vein markings, and its flowers grow in a loose cluster.

Some places along the AT you are likely to encounter one of the Rattlesnake Plantains: Between Timber Ridge Trail and Albert Mountain in North Carolina; on Thunder Ridge in central Virginia; and between Lions Head and Bear Mountain in Connecticut.

INDIAN PIPE

Monotropa uniflora

FLOWER:
Usually growing in small clumps, the nodding, nearly translucent flower is most often white, but it can also be pale shades of pink, yellow, or even blue.

BLOOM SEASON:
June to September

LEAVES AND STEM:
The leaves are nearly unnoticeable and are scalelike on a three- to ten-inch stem. Both the leaves and stem are the same color as the flower.

RANGE:
Georgia to Maine

From June into September (and sometimes even into October), search out and stop to study the unique Indian Pipe, which grows in heavily shaded areas. Although some recent research suggests Indian Pipe is in a symbiotic relationship with a fungus that grows on its roots, the plant has historically been recognized as being saprophytic, gaining its nourishment from decaying matter in the soil. Containing no chlorophyll (the substance that gives plants their green color), this herb rises from the soil on translucent, waxy-looking stems, and the pinkish white flower nods back toward the ground, giving the whole plant the appearance of a fancily carved soapstone pipe.

The genus name of *Monotropa*, meaning once-turned, refers to the plant's proclivity of lifting its head upright after producing seeds. Indian Pipe's ghostly color, its tendency to feel cold and turn black when touched, and the viscous fluid it oozes when its flesh has been broken, has given rise to a number of other common names such as Ghost Flower, Corpse Plant, Ice Plant, and Fairy Smoke.

Although it contains a poisonous substance, Indian Pipe has been used to treat eye problems, fainting spells, fevers, and—when combined with fennel—as a douche.

Pinesap (*Monotropa hypopithys*) is similar to Indian Pipe, but it has a reddish yellow tinge with several nodding flowers per stem. Sweet Pinesap (*Monotropsis odorata*) is much smaller, often hidden under forest litter, very fragrant, and only occurs from Georgia to Virginia/Maryland.

Some places along the AT you are likely to encounter Indian Pipe: Between Cheoah Bald and Stecoah Gap in North Carolina; on Catawba Mountain, and between Salt Log Gap and Fish Hatchery Road in central Virginia; on Peters Mountain in Pennsylvania; in Beartown and October Mountain State Forests, and on the slopes to Mount Greylock in Massachusetts; around Jeffers Brook Shelter in New Hampshire; and along Gulf Hagas Brook in Maine.

STARRY CAMPION

Silene stellata

FLOWER:

The five petals of Starry Campion grow in loose clusters atop slender stalks and are so deeply fringed that they sometimes look like many individual petals. The inflated, bell-shaped calyx is slightly hairy.

BLOOM SEASON:

June to September

LEAVES AND STEM:

The two- to four-inch, lance-shaped leaves are covered underneath with fine hair and occur in whorls of four along a stem two- to three-feet-high.

RANGE:

Georgia to Massachusetts

With an inclination for the environments of open woodlands, clearings, and thickets, and most often pollinated by moths and butterflies, Starry Campion, like many other plants, had a reputation for negating the effects of snake bites. However, the famous American field botanist, Dr. Asa Gray, made this report in 1842 after visiting the area around Grandfather Mountain in North Carolina:

"We had frequently been told of an antidote to the bite of the rattlesnake and copperhead—not unfrequent throughout the region—which is thought to possess wonderful efficacy, called Turman's snake-root, after an Indian doctor who had first employed it; the plant was brought to us by a man who was ready to attest to its virtues from his personal knowledge, and proved to be *Silene stellata*! Its use was suggested by the markings of the roots beneath the bark, in which these people find a fancied resemblance to the skin of the rattlesnake. Nearly all the reputed antidotes are equally inert; such herbs as *Impatiens pallida*, etc., being sometimes employed; so that we are led to conclude that the bite of these reptiles is seldom fatal, or even very dangerous in these cooler portions of the country."

In what seems to be quite a fanciful flight of the imagination, members of the genus *Silene* received their name from Silenus, the foster father of Bacchus of Greek mythology. Silenus was said to be fond of drink and was often found passed out, his face covered in the froth of beer. Evidently some observers were reminded of this foam when they looked at the sticky secretions found on several members of this genus.

Some places along the AT you are likely to encounter Starry Campion: Between Tesnatee Gap and Hogpen Gap in Georgia; in Yellow Mountain Gap in Tennessee; in the James River Face Wilderness, between Bryant Ridge and Floyd Mountain, and in the Humpback Rocks area in central Virginia.

WINTERGREEN

Gaultheria procumbens

For a small burst of refreshing flavor, chew on a leaf of Wintergreen. This is the plant whose oils have been used for centuries to flavor teas, medicines, candies, liniments, and chewing gum. (Interestingly, the same fragrant oil can be found in the twigs and sap of Yellow and Sweet Birch trees.)

Native Americans used extracts from the plant to lessen the pain of a headache or the discomforts of a fever. They must have known what they were doing, because Wintergreen contains methyl salicylate—or, as most of us call it, aspirin. Methyl salicylate has also been tested as an agent to slow the growth of tumors in human beings and used as an antiseptic and analgesic.

Also known as Teaberry or Checkerberry, Wintergreen is often found next to the trail growing on creeping stems and erect branches of two to six inches, with shiny, oval, evergreen leaves. New leaves appear before the flowers do; they become tinged with a pleasing hue of red during the colder months. The dangling, waxy, egg-shaped flowers are bisexual and are pollinated by insects. As summer progresses, they give rise to bright red berries which may stay on the plant throughout much of the year. Black bear and deer browse on the evergreen leaves during the winter, while ruffed grouse also appear to enjoy the fruit. The berries do have the pleasant taste of Wintergreen and have been added to salads and pies or eaten raw, but the flesh has a rather pithy and unpleasant texture.

Although sharing the same name, Wintergreen should not be confused with Spotted Wintergreen (*Chimaphila maculata;* see page 198).

Some places along the AT you are likely to encounter Wintergreen: Between Temple Hill Gap and the Nolichucky River in Tennessee; north of Matts Creek and south of Humpback Rocks in central Virginia; and between the Sandy River and Caribou Valley Road, and between ME 27 and Stratton Brook in Maine.

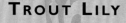

TROUT LILY

Erythronium americanum

FLOWER:
The nodding, one-and-a-half-inch, yellow flower has six petals and sepals that bend in a graceful, backward curve.

BLOOM SEASON:
March to May

LEAVES AND STEM:
The four- to six-inch elliptical leaves are mottled purple-brown and grow near the base of the six- to nine-inch stem.

RANGE:
Georgia to Maine

Like its western relative the Glacier Lily (*Erythronium grandiflorum*), Trout Lily is often found pushing its way through a blanket of snow in early spring; hikers at this time of year may come across a dense colony of them spreading out across the forest floor.

The plant originally received its common name from its leaves, which are speckled like the sides of a trout. Later on, people also liked to point out that it blooms during trout season. The leaves also provided another common name, Fawn Lily, because they stand straight up like the legs of a young deer and are spotted like a fawn's flanks. The protruding stamens of the flower caused some to call it Adder's-Tongue. Although not a true violet, the plant's pointed white corm is responsible for the name Dogtooth Violet.

If you are having foot problems while hiking the AT, you might be interested to know that Roman soldiers used the plant as a treatment for blisters and corns. In addition, if you ate something that disagreed with you, you should be aware that the leaves were boiled into a tea by Native Americans to relieve stomach cramps.

Botanists have only recently decided that another flower, also called Trout Lily, is a separate species (*Erythronium umbilicatum*) because it lacks the small, earlike appendages at the base of its petals, and the shape and orientation of its fruit is different from that of *Erythronium americanum*.

Some places along the AT you are likely to encounter Trout Lily: Between Deep Gap and Wallace Gap, and close to Walnut Mountain in North Carolina; around Little Bald on the North Carolina–Tennessee border; north of Virginia 624 and one mile north of Craig Creek in central Virginia; in low areas throughout Shenandoah National Park; along Conodoguinet Creek in Pennsylvania; around Bulls Bridge in Connecticut; on Moose Mountain in New Hampshire; and north of East B Hill Road in Maine.

LOUSEWORT

Pedicularis canadensis

FLOWER:
The three-quarter-inch flowers are composed of two petals that join together in tubular fashion. The upper lip is longer, has two, minute teeth, and arches downward over the shorter lower lip, which has three lobes. The flowers can be yellow or red, or a combination of both colors.

BLOOM SEASON:
April to June

LEAVES AND STEM:
The three- to five-inch, mostly basal leaves are sometimes reddish in color and are divided into such deeply toothed lobes that they almost look like fern fronds. A cushion of smaller leaves is just below the petals of the flower. The five- to fourteen-inch stem, as well as other parts of the plant, may be covered in fine hairs.

RANGE:
Georgia to Maine

Lousewort is one of the oddest-looking flowers found along the entire length of the AT. It could almost remind you of a plant from the primeval forest, what with its strangely shaped flower petals arranged above a supporting pad of small leaf bracts and its spreading basal leaves emulating the giant ferns of prehistoric times.

Adding to this primitive feeling, some sources point out that Lousewort is semiparasitic, as it derives some of its sustenance by stealing bits of nourishment from the roots of other plants. Other references state that Lousewort has a symbiotic relationship with a fungus that grows upon its roots and provides the plant with various nutrients.

The common name came into general usage centuries ago when farmers believed that their livestock would become infested with lice if the animals happened to graze through a patch of Lousewort. In fact, the genus name *Pedicularis* is derived from the Latin word for louse, *pediculus*.

Another common name, Wood Betony, is derived from the Latin *betonica*, meaning "herb." Some authorities speculate that this refers to a European herb that, during the Middle Ages, was believed to have wonderfully strong powers—such as keeping away evil spirits.

Swamp Lousewort (*Pedicularis lanceolata*) is not as common along the AT, but it does have a range from Georgia to southern New England, usually being found in wet meadows. Its appearance is similar, but its flowers are always yellow and its leaves are arranged oppositely on the twelve- to thirty-inch stem.

Some places along the AT you are likely to encounter one of the Louseworts: On Tray Mountain in Georgia; between Crawfish Valley and Walker Gap in southwest Virginia; on the north side of McAfee Knob in central Virginia; and north of Fernside Road in Massachusetts.

COMMON CINQUEFOIL

Potentilla simplex

FLOWER:

Rising on a single stem and looking somewhat like a small rose, the light-yellow, Common Cinquefoil flower has five petals and five large sepals. Some observers feel the flower resembles those of the wild strawberry.

BLOOM SEASON:

April to June

LEAVES AND STEM:

Leaves are divided into five radiating leaflets that are noticeably toothed. Each one rises on its own stalk from the hairy, horizontal runners.

RANGE:

Georgia to Maine

Common Cinquefoil thrives in poorer soils; along the AT you will most often see it in the disturbed ground alongside the pathway, growing on road banks, or in dry, open fields that are low in nutrients.

A number of Cinquefoils grow along the trail; two have the same range as the Common Cinquefoil. Canadian Dwarf Cinquefoil (*Potentilla canadensis*) is similar in appearance but has smaller leaves that are toothed only along their upper half. Rough-Fruited Cinquefoil (*Potentilla recta*), an import from Europe, is one of the largest of the genus with pale yellow, one-and-a-half-inch flowers that grow in a terminal cluster on a one- to two-foot stem. One of the country's rarest flowers, Dwarf Cinquefoil (*Potentilla robbinsiana*), like many other alpine plants, grows in small tufts and is covered in fine hairs, which help capture and retain moisture. Its flowers and leaflets are both no more than one-third of an inch in size. This exceptional species can be found along the slopes of Mount Washington in New Hampshire—the only spot in the United States where it grows.

Cinquefoils have had a colorful history. Witches were said to add them to their brew or to rub the plants on their bodies to produce trances. Medieval populations believed a tea made from the leaves would make a powerful love potion, while more practical people used the tea to treat mouth sores or to stop diarrhea. In her book, *Flowers and Their Histories*, Alice M. Coats says that the plant's five-fingered leaves came to represent the five senses; only knights that had the highest level of abilities and self-control were permitted to add Cinquefoil to their coat of arms.

Some places along the AT you are likely to encounter one of the Cinquefoils: On Wayah Bald in North Carolina; at Rice Field and Symms Gap in central Virginia; in Big Meadows in Shenandoah National Park; and between Little Swift River Pond Campsite and Spaulding Mountain, and at Crocker Cirque Campsite in Maine.

99

SQUAWROOT

Conopholis americana

The small, half-inch, yellowish to tan flowers have two lips, with the upper one forming a hood over a three-lobed, spreading lower lip.

April to June

Unconventional looking, the tannish yellow leaves of Squawroot are scalelike and crowded tightly onto a fleshy looking stalk three to nine inches high.

Georgia to Maine

A parasite upon the roots of trees—especially oaks—Squawroot has amazingly small yellow flowers. But the flower is probably not what will catch your eye at first. It will be the stem. The plant produces no chlorophyll—the substance that gives plants their green color—so its entire stem is sort of a yellowish brown.

In early spring you may come across a colony of Squawroot that has been scattered about and trampled upon. Most likely this is the result of black bears feeding upon the plants, as these animals—just having emerged from their winter slumbers—find the Squawroot to be some of the most delicious and abundant plants growing at that time of year.

Because the scalelike leaves make the plant resemble a pinecone, its generic name, *Conopholis*, is derived from Greek words meaning "cone" (*conos*) and "scale" (*pholis*). Its common name is probably in reference to it having been used by Native Americans in the treatment of menstrual disorders. Another common name is Cancer Root, but it should not be confused with other parasitic plants of the same name, such as One-Flowered Cancer Root (*Orobanche uniflora*) or Yellow Cancer Root (*Orobanche fasciculata*)—which more closely resembles Indian Pipe (*Monotropa uniflora*; see page 88). To confuse things even further, Black Cohosh (*Cimicifuga racemosa*) is sometimes referred to as Squawroot, because it, too, was used to alleviate the pains of menstruation.

Some places along the AT you are likely to encounter Squawroot: Chattahoochee Gap in Georgia; between Dicks Creek Gap in Georgia and Deep Gap in North Carolina; south of Scorched Earth Gap in central Virginia; and between Mount Mist and Jeffers Brook Shelter in New Hampshire.

WILD OATS

Uvularia sessilifolia

FLOWER:

The yellow, elongated, bell-shaped flowers are about one inch in length and droop (singly or in pairs from the leaf axils).

BLOOM SEASON:

May to June

LEAVES AND STEM:

The plant averages six to twelve inches in height, while the three-inch, lance-shaped leaves, light green above and whitish below, have no stems and are arranged oppositely.

RANGE:

Georgia to Maine

Wild Oats, also commonly referred to as Sessile Bellwort, is a member of the Bellwort family. Following the Doctrine of Signatures, herbalists once used Bellworts to treat throat ailments—the drooping flowers reminded them of the uvula, the flap of tissue that hangs from the soft palate at the back of the mouth. This also gave rise to the plant's genus name *Uvularia*. Its species name, *sessilifolia*, arises from the fact that its leaves are sessile, or without stems.

Once the flowers fade away and new leaves begin to appear, the plant takes on a new countenance as it becomes more expansive and stands almost erect.

Liking partial shade, rich soil, and moist conditions—an environment found along much of the AT—Wild Oats has a number of similar-looking relatives that may be seen up and down the trail. The stem of the Perfoliate Bellwort (*Uvularia perfoliata*) pierces the leaves that grow around its base, and the inside of the flower has rough, grainy, orange glands. Large-Flowered Bellwort (*Uvularia grandiflora*) grows up to twenty-four inches in height, has flowers up to two inches in length, and produces leaves covered underneath with a whitish down. Mountain Bellwort (*Uvularia pudica*), found only from Georgia to Virginia, most closely resembles Wild Oats, but its leaves are a brighter green and its stem is slightly downy.

The young shoots of almost all of these Bellworts have been cooked as a tasty substitute for asparagus. Native Americans taught early settlers how to make an emollient out of the plant to use on skin abscesses and wounds.

Some places along the AT you are likely to encounter one of the Bellworts: Between Rocky Mountain and Moreland Gap in Georgia; on Bluff Mountain along the North Carolina–Tennessee border; on the north slope of Pearis Mountain in southwest Virginia; between Thunder Hill and Petites Gap in central Virginia; south of Mosley Hill in Vermont; and north of East B Hill Road in Maine.

INDIAN CUCUMBER ROOT

Medeola virginiana

FLOWER:
   Emanating from the top whorl of leaves, the green-yellow, nodding flower's sepals and petals bend backwards.

BLOOM SEASON:
   May to June

LEAVES AND STEM:
   The unbranched, hairy stem grows from one to three feet tall and has two whorls of leaves, one set about halfway up and the other near the top.

RANGE:
   Georgia to Maine

Indian Cucumber Root, an intriguing-looking plant, rises on a single stem to a whorl of leaves about halfway up its length then continues rising to a second whorl on top. These uppermost leaves can hide the small, dangling, yellow flower. It is such a comely little flower that you should stop for a few moments to give it a thorough examination. Lifting it onto your fingers, you will notice that the three long stigmas curve gracefully back over the entire flower and are tinged a brownish red. The tiny stamens, which are close to the same color, stick straight out.

Later in the year, the leaves add dashes of color to the forest understory by turning red and offsetting the dark purple hues of the plant's small berries.

True to its name, the underground portion of the plant tastes a bit like cucumber and was part of Native American diets. But please refrain from trying a nibble of the root, as the plant is becoming more and more uncommon.

The Indian Cucumber Root is a member of the Lily family, which, among others, includes Ramps (*Allium tricoccum;* see page 76); Bluebead Lily (*Clintonia borealis;* see page 106); Turk's-Cap Lily (*Lilium superbum;* see page 120); the Solomon's Seals (genus *Polygonatum;* see page 42); the False Solomon's Seals (genus *Smilacina;* see page 48); and the Trilliums (genus *Trillium;* see pages 34 & 36). Botanists believe that the family includes 250 genera and close to 6,000 species worldwide.

Some places along the AT you are likely to encounter Indian Cucumber Root: North of Wayah Bald, and between Davenport Gap and Hot Springs in North Carolina; on The Priest in central Virginia; between Milesburn Road and Sandy Sod in Pennsylvania; on Mount Greylock in Massachusetts; between MA 2 and Seth Warner Shelter in Massachusetts and Vermont; and north of East B Hill Road in Maine.

BLUEBEAD LILY

Clintonia borealis

FLOWER:

Somewhat nodding, the one-inch-long flowers growing at the top of a six- to sixteen-inch stalk have three petals and three petal-like sepals that curve slightly backward.

BLOOM SEASON:

May to July

LEAVES AND STEM:

The basal, upright, oblong leaves are five to ten inches long.

RANGE:

Georgia to Maine

Favoring cool, moist woods with an acidic soil, Bluebead Lily is most common in the evergreen forests of the northern AT states, though it can be found in abundant colonies in the spruce-fir forests of the south—such as those in the Great Smokies along the North Carolina–Tennessee border or on Apple Orchard Mountain and at other high elevations in Virginia. This penchant for chilly environments is reflected in its species name, *borealis.* The plant's genus name, *Clintonia*, honors Dewitt Clinton, a governor of New York and a noted amateur naturalist of his day. This also accounts for another common name, Yellow Clintonia.

The most striking aspect of the Bluebead Lily is not its flowers, but its leaves. Each plant has two or three, richly green, basal leaves that are broadly oval-shaped, have tiny hairs along their margins, and can be ten inches or longer in length. When young, the leaves taste a bit like cucumbers and can be used in salads. Late in the summer the flowers develop into the rich blue berries which give the plant its name. These berries may look delicious and inviting, but be aware that they are slightly poisonous.

Native Americans used the plant to treat burns, infections, and problems of the heart, and they gave it to women to help reduce the pain of childbirth. Modern science has found the rootstock to contains an anti-inflammatory, proving that some treatments in folk medicine are accurate.

Some places along the AT you are likely to encounter Bluebead Lily: On Apple Orchard Mountain in central Virginia; between Mount Greylock and Mount Fitch in Massachusetts; between MA 2 and Seth Warner Shelter in Massachusetts and Vermont; on Glastenbury Mountain in Vermont; between Mount Jackson and Mizpah Spring Hut, between Lowe's Bald Spot and Pinkham Notch, and on the south end of Wildcat Mountain in New Hampshire; and north of East B Hill Road and along Stratton Brook in Maine.

WHORLED LOOSESTRIFE

Lysimachia quadrifolia

FLOWER:

Borne on threadlike stalks that emanate from the leaf axils, the small, star-shaped, yellow blossoms of the Whorled Loosestrife have a bit of red in their centers (which may radiate outward in thin lines). The one pistil extends beyond the five stamens.

BLOOM SEASON:

Late May to August

LEAVES AND STEM:

The light green, lanceolate leaves grow in whorls—usually of four—along the stem, which reaches heights of one to three feet.

RANGE:

Georgia to Maine

A long-lasting bloomer (blooming from May to August), Whorled Loosestrife grows as a common plant in open woodlands, clearings, fields, and thickets. It appears to be spreading rapidly throughout its range.

Sources give differing accounts as to how the plant received its genus name. Some say *Lysimachia* is derived from the Greek word *lusimakhos*, which can be loosely translated to mean "ending strife." A much more colorful theory relates the story of Lysimachus, the King of Sicily, who upon being chased by a raging bull, waved a Loosestrife in front of the animal—which calmed it down. Based upon this tale, early American settlers fed Whorled Loosestrife to their oxen and placed the plant in the animals' yokes, so that the livestock would work together more peacefully and would be easier to handle.

As a rebuff to Great Britain and a rejection of the tea tax, colonists refused to drink commercial tea. Instead, they brewed what they called Liberty Tea, made from the leaves of Loosestrifes. If your feet have swollen from too much hard-and-fast hiking, you may be interested to know crushed Loosestrife leaves have been used to treat injuries inflicted by boots that are too tight.

Whorled Loosestrife is an example of how confusing common names can be. It and other members of the genus *Lysimachia*—such as Fringed Loosestrife (*Lysimachia ciliata*) and Lance-Leaved Loosestrife (*Lysimachia lanceolata*)—are not true Loosestrifes, but are members of the Primrose family. True Loosestrifes include only the genus *Lythrum*, such as Spiked (or Purple) Loosestrife (*Lythrum salicaria*).

Some places along the AT you are likely to encounter one of the Loosestrifes: Near the spring for Campbell Shelter, on the side trail to Sunset Field, and south of Punchbowl Shelter in central Virginia; in Michaux State Forest in Pennsylvania; and south of Mount Race in Massachusetts.

GRAY'S LILY

Lilium grayi

The nodding, two-and-one-half-inch flowers of the Gray's Lily grow either solitarily or in groups of up to twelve at the end of the stem. The orange-red blossoms are heavily marked with purple spots. Their pointed petals flare outward, but, unlike many other lilies, do not bend backwards.

June to July

The lanceolate leaves occur in whorls along the stem, which reaches heights of two to four feet. The leaves are a bit rough on the undersides of the veins.

North Carolina/Tennessee to southwest Virginia

Sometimes the AT's protected corridor helps preserve habitat for rare, threatened, or endangered plants, as is the case for the June- to July-blooming Gray's Lily. Named for Dr. Asa Gray, the famous American botanist, this lily is sometimes referred to as the Roan Lily after the mountain on which Dr. Gray first discovered the plant in 1840.

He collected the flower and preserved it in his herbarium at Cambridge University. At the time, Dr. Gray considered it to be the Canada Lily (*Lilium canadense*), which it strongly resembles (and which has a range along the AT from Georgia and North Carolina to Maine). However, on a return trip to the mountains in 1879, he collected additional samples, and it was then that Dr. Sereno Watson studied the plant and found it to have enough distinctive traits to be its own species.

As far as research can determine, Gray's Lily rarely appears anywhere else on the AT except on Roan Mountain, a few of its neighboring balds along the North Carolina–Tennessee border, and in the open meadows around the highlands of the Mount Rogers area in southwest Virginia. (The Appalachian Trail Conservancy is involved in a continuing study trying to determine where and what other types of rare, threatened, or endangered plants may happen to grow within the trail's corridor and how to best protect them.)

Some places along the AT you are likely to encounter Gray's Lily: On Hump, Yellow, and Roan Mountains and other nearby balds on the North Carolina–Tennessee border; and on Whitetop Mountain in southwest Virginia.

III

SUNDROPS

Oenothera fruticosa

FLOWER:

The flowers rise from a single stem and have four petals and a pistil whose top (the stigma) is shaped like a cross.

BLOOM SEASON:

June to August

LEAVES AND STEM:

The lanceolate leaves are arranged alternately on a hairy stem two to three feet high.

RANGE:

Georgia to Maine

You may have the occasion while hiking on the AT to make a base camp for a couple of days close to a small patch of Sundrops. What a wonderful opportunity you have if you happen to find yourself in this situation! Fight off the urge to stay snug and comfortable in your sleeping bag and rouse yourself to emerge from your tent at about the same time the early morning light begins to spread across the distant ridgelines.

Be sure to keep an eye on the Sundrops while you prepare breakfast, and you will be treated to one of the natural world's small dances. The tightly wound, reddish orange, tapering buds will begin to spread outward, eventually opening up to become deep-golden blossoms whose pigment mimics that of the solar orb rising higher into the sky.

You might forget all about the plants as you head out for a day hike to a grand vista or a crashing waterfall, but when you return to camp in early evening, the blossoms will still be there. Yet, as your stove begins to boil your dinner water and the shadows from the surrounding vegetation begin to lengthen, you cannot help but notice that the flowers are folding up, as if retiring for the day and preparing for the cooler night air.

Just before bedding down for your own slumbers, make a mental note of which particular Sundrops have blossoms and where the flowers are arranged on the plants. When you arise tomorrow morning, the blooms you watched today will probably have withered away, and new ones will help you greet the promise of a fresh dawn.

Some places along the AT you are likely to encounter Sundrops: Along the side trail to Whitley Gap Shelter in Georgia; and south of Brickey's Gap and in Black Horse Gap in central Virginia.

SPOTTED JEWELWEED

Impatiens capensis

FLOWER:
The almost-one-inch, hanging, orange flowers are spurred and spotted with small reddish brown dots. The lowest of the three sepals curls to the back and makes a sac with a spur.

BLOOM SEASON:
June to September

LEAVES AND STEM:
The plant grows two to five feet tall and has leaves that are two to five inches long, toothed, and somewhat elliptical in shape.

RANGE:
Georgia to Maine

Because they tend to favor the same environment, Jewelweed and Stinging Nettle (*Urtica dioica*) are often found growing side by side in large patches lining the pathway. Brushing up against the Stinging Nettle will give its tiny, stiff hairs an opportunity to scratch your skin and deposit an irritant that will often itch for the rest of the day. One experience of this kind will keep you on the watch for the Nettle. Luckily, the Jewelweed's succulent stems contain a juice that helps ease the Nettle's sting when rubbed over the itching areas of your skin.

If you look closely at these plants, you will note that their tops have been nipped off at an almost uniform height. Both the Jewelweed and Stinging Nettle are favorite foods of the deer, but the animals will stop feeding upon the plants at the point it becomes uncomfortable for them to bend any further. This point is known as the "browse line." In years of scarce food, the browse line may be lower than normal as the deer continue to eat downward to obtain any nourishment they can.

Also commonly found along the trail is Pale Jewelweed (*Impatiens pallida*), which ranges from Georgia to Maine. Its flowers are pale yellow and larger than Spotted Jewelweed, but the spur is shorter. The blossoms may have only a few spots or none at all.

In the fall you can find out why Jewelweed is also known as Touch-Me-Not or Snapweed. When its seed pods are good and ripe, just touching them will cause them to explode open, casting the seeds in various directions.

Some places along the AT you are likely to encounter one of the Jewelweeds: Between Carter Gap Shelter and Big Spring Shelter in North Carolina; along Thunder Hill and near Cow Camp Shelter in central Virginia; on Mount Greylock in Massachusetts; in wet areas on the slopes of Killington Peak and beside Kent Pond in Vermont; and along moist stream areas in New Hampshire.

BLACK-EYED SUSAN

Rudbeckia hirta

FLOWER:

The flower of the Black-Eyed Susan is quite complex. The blossom grows at the end of a single stem, and its center cone is made up of hundreds of small florets which produce seeds and bloom in a ring around the cone. Connected to the cone and radiating outward are ten to twenty, long, orange-yellow rays.

BLOOM SEASON:

June to October

LEAVES AND STEM:

The two- to seven-inch leaves are lance-shaped (but may be a bit ovate), have distinct veins, and grow alternately on a stem of one to three feet in height. Both the leaves and the stem are slightly hairy.

RANGE:

Georgia to Maine

Black-Eyed Susans are a perfect example of how humans affect the makeup of the natural world. Not native to the eastern United States, they were originally found only in the plains and prairie lands of North America. It is believed the flower made its way to the AT states in the 1830s when its seeds became mixed with shipments of red clover seeds—which eastern farmers were eager to plant in their fields because its roots have bacteria that add nutrients to the soil. Today Black-Eyed Susans are found in nearly every state in the United States and in many Canadian provinces.

As it can now be found in every state along the trail—and because it blooms from June into October—the Black-Eyed Susan is a plant that will accompany AT thru-hikers throughout most of their journey, whether they are walking northward or southward. Favoring dry fields, open woods, waste areas, and roadsides, the individual blossoms are long-lasting, staying healthy and blooming for nearly a month when conditions are right.

The plant is very prolific because it has a number of ways in which it insures its propagation. Its bright color attracts large numbers of insects and its wealth of pollen is easily harvested by those with short tongues. Those with longer tongues, such as butterflies, moths, and bees, are able to reach into the flower tubes to obtain the nectar. As a deterrent to unwanted invaders such as ants, the stem of the Black-Eyed Susan is covered in small barblike projections, which make it nearly impossible for any crawling insect to climb up and reach the flower.

Some places along the AT you are likely to encounter Black-Eyed Susans: Between Beech Gap and Big Spring Shelter in North Carolina; south of Street Gap along the North Carolina–Tennessee border; in the meadows near VA 42 and Catawba Creek in central Virginia; on numerous Skyline Drive crossings in Shenandoah National Park; and along MA 41 at South Egremont in Massachusetts.

BUTTER-AND-EGGS

Linaria vulgaris

Originally a native of Asia, Butter-and-Eggs was introduced into the United States from Europe and can now be found in temperate zones throughout the world. Its success at propagating itself can be traced to a number of factors.

Its orange color attracts many insects, especially those bumblebees and honeybees that are strong enough to open the flower's lip and are large enough to reach inside the tube to obtain the nectar. While doing this, they rub against the stamen, which drops pollen onto their bodies. Once fertilized, one flower can be the progenitor of many new plants, as each blossom is able to produce a prodigious amount of seeds. In addition, Butter-and-Eggs is able to send up new shoots from its spreading rhizomes; this is why you may often find the plant growing in large colonies.

The genus name of *Linaria* is related to the word, *linum*, which is Latin for "flax" and refers to the fact that the leaves of Butter-and-Eggs resemble those of the flax plant. This, in turn, leads to another common name, Yellow Toadflax. (The toad in this name is in reference to how the flower opens its mouth like a toad when it is squeezed.)

Incidentally, in his highly informative book, *Hedgemaids and Fairy Candles*, Jack Sanders states that he has come across more than thirty different common names for Butter-and-Eggs. Among the most colorful are Patten and Clogs, Lion's Mouth, Devil's Head, Eggs-and-Collops, Eggs-and-Bacon, Bread-and-Butter, Calve's Snout, Impudent Lawyer, Deadman's Bones, Fluellin, Dragon Bushes, and Churnstaff.

Some places along the AT you are likely to encounter Butter-and-Eggs: On Max Patch in North Carolina; between Black Horse Gap and Bear Wallow Gap, and on Cold Mountain in central Virginia; along Perkins Drive in New York; in fields next to Schaghticoke Road in Connecticut; and in meadows along the Housatonic River in Massachusetts.

TURK'S-CAP LILY

Lilium superbum

FLOWER:

The large (five inches in diameter), orange, nodding flowers have three petals and three sepals of the same size and color that curve sharply backward. A green line at the base of each forms a star where they meet. The projecting stamens are tipped with dangling anthers.

BLOOM SEASON:

July to August

LEAVES AND STEM:

The lanceolate leaves grow in whorls along a stem three to seven feet high.

RANGE:

Georgia to southern New England

By far one of the largest of the wildflowers along the AT, the Turk's-Cap Lily stands out as a notably colorful flower in the mid- to late summer forest. This showy plant puts on a wonderful display, having as many as forty individual flowers blooming at the same time, all nodding their heads downward and swinging slightly from side to side in response to the lightest of breezes.

Its species name of *superbum* means "superb" and is an acknowledgment of the plant's glamour and charm. The common name comes from the fact that the flower's backward curving petals and sepals are thought to resemble a martagân, a turban-like cap worn by Turks in centuries past.

Carolina Lily (*Lilium michauxii*), which ranges from Georgia to Virginia/West Virginia, looks very similar, but generally only has one to three flowers on a shorter stem. The blossoms are also smaller and usually lack the green "star." The leaves are thicker, a bit whitish, and broadest near the tip.

The Tiger Lily (*Lilium tigrinum*) is a native of eastern Asia, but has escaped from gardens in the United States and has begun to establish itself locally in the wild. Although its flowers are similar to the Turk's-Cap Lily, its leaves do not grow in whorls, but are arranged alternately along the stem and have bulblets (small, fleshy orbs) in their axils.

A Greek legend holds that Lilies developed from the drops of milk that fell from the sky as the goddess Juno was nursing her half-god/half-human son, Hercules.

Some places along the AT you are likely to encounter Turk's-Cap Lily: South of Gooch Gap and in Henry Gap in Georgia; north and south of Bly Gap, and between Beech Gap and Big Spring Shelter in North Carolina; on Apple Orchard Mountain, Bald Knob, and The Priest in central Virginia; and throughout Shenandoah National Park.

YELLOW-FRINGED
ORCHID

Habenaria ciliaris

FLOWER:

Growing in large terminal clusters, the flowers of the Yellow-Fringed Orchid have a lower lip that is deeply fringed and can be almost three-quarters of an inch in length. A long, slim spur of one and a half inches extends backward and downward from the base of the flower.

BLOOM SEASON:

July to September

LEAVES AND STEM:

The leaves are lanceolate and sheath the stem, which may reach a height of two feet. The lower leaves can grow to be ten inches long, while the upper ones are much shorter.

RANGE:

Georgia to New York (every once in a while, Yellow-Fringed Orchid is found in southern New England, but it is a rare occurrence)

Once you spot Yellow-Fringed Orchids as you struggle up a steep slope while hiking during the heat of an August afternoon, you may wish you had never seen them. Their milky orange-yellow flowers may make your mouth water, as they can't help but remind you of what a treat a Creamsicle—that refreshingly frozen treat of orange sherbet and vanilla ice cream—would be for your sweating body.

To the early settlers of the southern mountains, the plant resembled a rattlesnake—the fringed lip suggested the shape of a serpent's forked tongue while the anther sacs looked like fangs. Despite a general belief in the Doctrine of Signatures, it does not appear that the mountaineers used the plant as a treatment for snake bites.

The Yellow-Fringed Orchid has a tendency to favor peaty soils and grassy bogs, but can also be found thriving in sandy soils, in open woodlands, or on dry hillsides and meadows.

Ranging from Georgia to Pennsylvania/New Jersey, but seen much less often along the trail, the Orange-Fringed Orchid (*Habenaria cristata*) has smaller flowers with shorter lips and spurs, while the leaves are narrower, more pointed and fewer in number. Since these orchids sometimes cross-fertilize and hybridize, it may be hard to tell just exactly which species you have come across.

When looking to other sources for further information about the Yellow-Fringed Orchid, you should be aware that some reference books follow the classifications of John T. Kartesz and place the flower within the genus *Platanthera*.

Some places along the AT you are likely to encounter Yellow-Fringed Orchid: Between Tellico Gap and Wesser Bald in North Carolina.

TALL GOLDENROD

Solidago altissima

FLOWER:
Arranged in showy clusters along the upper branches, the individual flowers are small, not much more than one-quarter of an inch in size.

BLOOM SEASON:
August to November

LEAVES AND STEM:
The lanceolate leaves, which may be up to six inches in length, are arranged alternately on the three- to seven-foot stem.

RANGE:
Most common from Georgia to New York, but may also be found in New England

Close to one hundred kinds of Goldenrods inhabit North America, with nearly fifty species found in New England alone. The distinctions between them are sometimes so slight that even the most expert of botanists have become perplexed and given up, saying that a particular plant is simply "a goldenrod." Hybridization only adds to this complexity of identification.

There are two species along the trail which share the same range and look almost identical to *Solidago altissima*. Canada Goldenrod (*Solidago canadensis*) has leaves that are noticeably toothed and its flowers are smaller, while the blossoms of the Late Goldenrod (*Solidago gigantea*) have a whitish tinge to them.

Some of the most conspicuous of the late summer and autumn flowers, Goldenrods are estimated to be visited by more than one hundred species of insects, including the bumblebee and the praying mantis. This plant is often blamed for causing the discomforts of hayfever. However, the Goldenrod's pollen is quite sticky. Instead of wafting into the air and into your nose at every mild breeze, it stays on the plants until picked up by visiting insects. The true culprit of the human malady is Ragweed, which blooms at about the same time and whose minute particles of pollen are easily blown by the slightest of winds.

Because they contain a small amount of rubber, Thomas Edison once theorized that Goldenrods could be an economical source for the substance; modern day experiments with hybridization are beginning to show promise.

Some places along the AT you are likely to encounter one of the Goldenrods: At Doll Flats in North Carolina; near the New River, and between Reeds Gap and Rockfish Gap in central Virginia; throughout Shenandoah National Park (especially Skyline Drive crossings); many road crossings in Connecticut; and along Hubbard Brook in Massachusetts.

PINK TO RED FLOWERS

ROUND-LOBED HEPATICA

Hepatica americana

FLOWER:
Lacking petals, these nearly one-inch flowers have five to nine sepals which range from white to pink to lilac or even to lavender-blue. Numerous stamens have pale anthers, while a small cluster of pistils lies at the center of the flower. Just below the flower are three green leaf bracts.

BLOOM SEASON:
March to May

LEAVES AND STALK:
The two-inch-wide, three-lobed leaves grow from the base of the hairy stems.

RANGE:
Georgia to Maine

Found up and down the trail, Hepatica's appearance—along with, or soon after, Spring Beauty's (*Claytonia virginica;* see page 128)—was once used by farmers as a guide to when they could safely plant their crops and avoid a late frost. A member of the Buttercup family, it is often found blooming in the same place and at the same time as its relatives, the Anemones.

Also known as Liverwort, the Round-Lobed Hepatica flower is self-fertilizing. This is probably an adaptation based on its early blooming season; insects that could aid in pollination are few and far between so early in the year. Interestingly, some flowers contain a scent while others do not—and this may change from year to year. Most often, the white blossoms will be the most heavily scented. But in some years, the blue blossoms—which may have had no smell the previous blooming season—will be the ones with the most pleasant aroma.

The plant's genus name, *Hepatica*, is derived from the Greek word for liver, because its leaves remain on the stem throughout the winter and dry into a rusty, liverlike color. Coupled with the leaf's three-lobed resemblance to the organ, herb doctors, following the Doctrine of Signatures, used the plant as a treatment for liver problems.

More common in the central United States than along the AT, Sharp-Lobed Hepatica (*Hepatica acutiloba*) has a similar appearance, but its leaf bracts and lobes are more pointed. Some botanists claim that Sharp-Lobed Hepatica is just a race, or subspecies, of Round-Lobed Hepatica.

Some places along the AT you are likely to encounter one of the Hepaticas: On Fork Mountain in central Virginia; below Fishers Gap Overlook in Shenandoah National Park; south of Bulls Bridge in Connecticut; north of Fernside Road in Massachusetts; and around the vicinity of Velvet Rocks in New Hampshire.

SPRING BEAUTY

Claytonia virginica

True to their name, Spring Beauties are some of the first flowers to emerge as the weather gets just a bit warmer from the cold of winter. These pinkish white flowers sometimes line the AT in such great quantities that they appear to be patches of slowly melting snow.

The flowers, which usually only last about three days, are bisexual, but the female and male parts mature at different times, preventing self-pollination.

Deer and moose browse on the tiny flowers and leaves, while chipmunks, mice, and many people—Native Americans and the early settlers in the past, and even some people today—have found the root of the plant to be quite delectable and nutritious. Tasting like radishes when raw, the roots have been likened to potatoes with a sweet, chestnut-like flavor when baked or boiled in soups or stews.

The Spring Beauty holds quite an interest to geneticists. While most organisms of the same species have the same number of chromosomes (humans have forty-six), the number in the Spring Beauty varies from plant to plant with more than fifty chromosomal combinations having been discovered in different individuals.

A relative, the Carolina Spring Beauty (*Claytonia caroliniana*), has a similar appearance, but its leaves are wider and its habitat is usually a slightly drier environment.

Some places along the AT you are likely to encounter one of the Spring Beauties: Between Unicoi Gap and Dicks Creek Gap in Georgia; between Indian Gap and Newfound Gap in the Great Smoky Mountains National Park, and on Bluff Mountain and Big Bald on the North Carolina–Tennessee border; on Pearis Mountain in southwest Virginia; on Peters Mountain in central Virginia; on the slopes of Mount Greylock in Massachusetts; and between Clearwater Brook and the Sandy River, and near Moxie Pond in Maine.

PINK AZALEA

Rhododendron nudiflorum

FLOWER:
The pistils and stamens project far out from the five petals of the two-inch-wide, pink, trumpet-shaped flowers.

BLOOM SEASON:
March to May

LEAVES AND STEM:
The yellowish green leaves are long and become narrow at each end. Unlike the evergreen leaves of some members of the Heath family, the Pink Azalea's leaves are deciduous.

RANGE:
Georgia to Massachusetts

A flower that truly makes a spring hike along the AT a thing of beauty, the Pink Azalea, also known as Pinxter-Flower or Wild Azalea, grows on shrubs that can reach eight feet in height. The habit of blossoming out before the leaves appear gave the plant its species name, *nudiflorum*, basically translating as "coming into flower while still naked."

In late spring you may notice a golf-ball-sized growth at the end of a Pink Azalea twig. This gall-like form is produced by a bacteria or fungus and, surprisingly, is quite tasty. In fact, this little sweet was so highly prized in earlier times that it was preserved and saved as a treat for later in the year.

Similar in appearance to Pink Azalea but with very fragrant flowers, Early Azalea (*Rhododendron roseum*)—ranging from Virginia to Maine—can be found between Humpback Mountain and Humpback Rocks in central Virginia and on many of the dry, south-facing slopes of Connecticut. Another relative with pink or magenta flowers, but with stamens and pistils almost completely exposed, Rhodora (*Rhododendron canadense*)—ranging from Pennsylvania to Maine—brightens the bog just south of Carl Newhall Lean-To in Maine. The white blossoms of Swamp Azalea (*Rhododendron viscosum*)—ranging from Georgia to Maine—are most often seen along the AT in the wetlands of New Jersey and New York. With rich orange flowers, the Flame Azalea (*Rhododendron calendulaceum;* see page 198)—ranging from Georgia to Pennsylvania—grows well on the southern slopes of Tray Mountain in Georgia, and between Humpback Mountain and Humpback Rocks in central Virginia.

Some places along the AT you are likely to encounter Pink Azalea: Along the ridgeline of Pearis Mountain in southwest Virginia; in Bear Wallow Gap and between Humpback Mountain and Humpback Rocks in central Virginia; between Jenkins Gap and Compton Springs in Shenandoah National Park; and between Lions Head and Bear Mountain in Connecticut.

WILD GERANIUM

Geranium maculatum

FLOWER:
The pink to purplish, upright, round-petaled flowers have five pointed sepals, ten stamens, and one pistil. They grow in loose clusters of two to five.

BLOOM SEASON:
April to June

LEAVES AND STEM:
The grayish leaves have coarsely toothed lobes and grow oppositely on a stem one to two feet in height. They may become covered with white dots as they age.

RANGE:
Georgia to Maine

Because the plant is bisexual—its flowers go through male and female stages—Wild Geranium cannot self-pollinate. Individual flowers last one to three days; by the time the female organs have developed and are ready to be fertilized, the pollen-producing anthers of the male have faded away. (When conditions are right, a flower may change from a male to a female in a few hours.) Since the flower needs to become fertilized quickly, it is believed that the darker purple lines along its petals help guide insects to the nectar.

After the pink and purplish petals of the Wild Geranium drop off, an elongated ovary becomes part of the seed pod, which resembles a bird's head with a long beak rising up from the stem. In fact, hundreds of years ago inhabitants of the Old World named the plant Cranesbill, and even the word geranium comes from the Greek *geranos*, which means "crane." As the seeds ripen and enlarge, they cause the pod to curl and become ever tighter. Eventually the pressure becomes too much and the pod bursts, sending the seeds out in all directions. Some observers say the seeds are catapulted more than thirty feet away.

As all parts of the Wild Geranium contain tannin, it was once used as an astringent. In fact, the plant has so many medicinal uses that it was listed in the *United States Pharmacopoeia* for nearly a hundred years. Sore throats, influenza, mouth sores, swollen feet, stomach disorders, hemorrhoids, gonorrhea, and more were said to be successfully treated by using the plant to make up various concoctions.

Some places along the AT you are likely to encounter Wild Geranium: Between Wine Spring and A. Rufus Morgan Shelter, and between High Rocks and Spivey Gap in North Carolina; north of Angel's Rest in southwest Virginia; between Punchbowl Shelter and Johns Hollow, on The Priest, and along Humpback Mountain in central Virginia; in moist areas near Lions Head in Connecticut; and the lower slopes of Jug End in Massachusetts.

SHOWY ORCHIS

Orchis spectabilis

FLOWER:

Emanating from the axils of the leaf bracts, several of Showy Orchis' blossoms are arranged along a four- to twelve-inch-high flower spike. Each flower is about one inch long, has three sepals, two lateral petals that form a purple to pink hood, and a lower white lip with a spur hanging from it.

BLOOM SEASON:

April to June

LEAVES AND STEM:

Enveloping the bottom of the flower stalk are two widely ovate basal leaves. Each smooth leaf is about four to eight inches long.

RANGE:

Georgia to Maine

Found most often in rich, moist woodlands or along the edges of swamps and bogs, the Showy Orchis is fertilized by bumblebees that visit the flower to feast upon the abundant nectar found inside its tube. Elsewhere on the blossom, the spur of the lower lip contains a sweet syrup high in sugar content. (It should be noted that sometimes the lower lip is pink, while in some variants the entire flower is white.)

The genus name *Orchis* comes from the Greek word *orkhis*, meaning "testicles," and refers to some of the plants' roots, which are rounded and fleshy and apparently reminded past observers of the shape of a man's gonads. Following the Doctrine of Signatures, this observation gave rise to the notion that the plant was a powerful aphrodisiac. In fact, the ancient Greeks believed just holding the bulbs could arouse desire and enhance sexual performance.

The Greeks were not the only ones who ascribed such potent powers to this genus of plants. The Romans called the flowers "satyrion," believing the plant had its origins in the semen spilled by the mythical (and sexually powerful) satyrs. The English variously called it "fool's ballocks," "hares ballocks," and "goat stones." One other name was "sweet cods" (*cod* being Old English for scrotum). (If you can remember back to your high school days and readings of Shakespeare's plays, you may recall coming across a reference to a codpiece, which was a flap of material that was, functionally, the precursor of the zipper.)

When looking to other sources for further information about Showy Orchis, you should be aware that some reference books follow the classifications of John T. Kartesz and list the plant as *Galearis spectabilis*.

Some places along the AT you are likely to encounter Showy Orchis: In the Great Smoky Mountains National Park; between High Rocks and Spivey Gap in North Carolina; and on Thunder Ridge, and between Long Mountain Wayside and Pedlar Lake in central Virginia.

FIRE PINK

Silene virginica

FLOWER:

The unmistakable, richly scarlet, one- to two-inch flowers have five petals that are notched—sometimes deeply. Several may grow on thin stalks from the axils of the upper leaves.

BLOOM SEASON:

April to June

LEAVES AND STEM:

The long (up to five inches) basal leaves are opposite; the plant often attains a height of one to two feet.

RANGE:

Georgia to New York

One of the brightest and most conspicuous wildflowers found blooming in the Appalachian Mountains, the Fire Pink is also one of the longer lasting flowers, blooming from sometime in April well into June. The pink in the name refers not to the color of the flower, but rather to the notch at the end of each petal; the notch looks like the ragged or serrated edge of sewing material cut by pinking shears. Field observations seem to bear out that Fire Pinks growing in the southern AT states appear more deeply notched, with petals that are narrower and more pointed, than those found further north.

This plant has tiny hairs covered in a sticky substance along the length of its stem that capture insects to prevent them from reaching the flower's nectar. Because of these tiny hairs, Fire Pink is sometimes commonly referred to as Catchfly. Yet, the brilliant red of the flower is a natural attractant to hummingbirds, which are often seen flitting from plant to plant, dipping their long beaks into the flowers' narrow tubes, enjoying their sweet juices.

Described elsewhere in this book are other members of the Pink family, most of which also have notches in their petals. Deptford Pink (*Dianthus armeria;* see page 148) ranges from Georgia to Maine. Starry Campion (*Silene stellata;* see page 90) can be found from Georgia to Massachusetts, while Star Chickweed (*Stellaria pubera;* see page 14) occurs from Georgia to New Jersey. Rare in the south, Mountain Sandwort (*Arenaria groenlandica;* see page 70) clings to the higher elevations from Georgia to New York but is a bit more common on the rocky ridges of New England.

Some places along the AT you are likely to encounter Fire Pink: Between Springer Mountain and Stover Creek in Georgia; between Betty Creek Gap and Bear Pen Trail, between Wallace Gap and Siler Bald, and between Wesser Bald and Wesser in North Carolina; and north of VA 311, and along The Priest in central Virginia.

COLUMBINE

Aquilegia canadensis

FLOWER:
The Columbine's flower is a nodding red and yellow blossom, one to two inches in size, with five petals curving upwards as hollow spurs.

BLOOM SEASON:
April to July

LEAVES AND STEM:
The leaves are compound, divided into three, and grow on a one- to two-foot stem.

RANGE:
Georgia to Maine

At some time in the distant past, Columbine's ornate and unusual flowers reminded people of flocks of hovering birds, and the plant earned the name *columba*, Latin for "dove." Some sources say that its five, long, curving spurs resemble an eagle's talons and resulted in the plant's genus name *Aquilegia*, derived from Latin for "eagle." Others claim the name comes from the Latin, *aqua* for "water" and *legere* for "collect," which would refer to the sweet liquid nectar that collects in the spurs.

Look closely at the spurs and you may see tiny holes in the tips. Most bees and many other insects are too large to gain access to the nectar by crawling into the spurs; they simply nip the tip and steal the nectar without collecting any pollen. But the flower's red color entices hummingbirds, whose needle-like bills and long tongues enable them to reach the nectar at the base of the spurs, making them the Columbine's most efficient pollinators.

In the past, the juice from a fresh Columbine plant was given to those suffering from jaundice to help reduce the size of a swollen liver. The leaves and flowers were also believed to cure measles and small pox. Columbine may not have cured these ills, but since the plant does contain prussic acid, it may have had a narcotic and soothing effect which helped ease sufferer's pains.

Some places along the AT you are likely to encounter Columbine: Between the Nolichucky River in Tennessee and Damascus in Virginia; on Sinking Creek Mountain, near High Cock Knob, and around Bald Knob in central Virginia; along the Housatonic River in Connecticut; around Jug End in Massachusetts; and along the Moose Mountain ridgeline in New Hampshire.

PINK LADY'S SLIPPER

Cypripedium acaule

FLOWER:

The upper two petals are long and slender and range from yellow-green to purple-brown. It is the other petal, though, that makes this plant so distinctive. It is one to three inches long, bulbous in shape, richly pink, marked with darker pink to red veins, and it folds to a deep cleft in the middle.

BLOOM SEASON:

Late April to July

LEAVES AND STEM:

Two, broad, four- to eight-inch leaves grow from the base of a stem that rises six to twenty-four inches high.

RANGE:

Georgia to Maine

Like other orchids, the exotic structure of the Pink Lady's Slipper, also known as Moccasin Flower, is designed to attract certain pollinators. After insects work their way through the slit in the red-veined pouch, they deposit pollen from other plants by brushing against the stigma. Exiting the flower by way of the two openings at the rear of the slipper, the insects then pick up that plant's pollen by grazing the anthers. These plants need more than this process to reproduce though. In common with other members of the Orchid family, Lady's Slippers will only grow when certain fungi are present in their roots. If soil and weather conditions are not conducive to the growth of the fungi, the Lady's Slipper will not survive.

Although it is rarely ever seen, the Showy Lady's Slipper (*Cypripedium reginae*) has a range that covers almost the entire route of the AT. The largest of the Lady's Slippers, its petals and sepals are a pure white, while the pouch is tinged with a pinkish rose hue. The pouch is also marked with dots or lines of deep magenta. The much smaller Yellow Lady's Slipper (*Cypripedium calceolus;* see page 198) also ranges from Georgia to Maine.

The admonishment to not pick any wildflowers along the trail is even stronger with the Lady's Slippers, since they appear to become more rare with each passing year.

Some places along the AT you are likely to encounter one of the Lady's Slippers: Between Davenport Gap and Hot Springs in North Carolina; south of Crawfish Valley in southwest Virginia; between Bear Wallow Gap and Parkers Gap Road, along Thunder Hill, and on Bluff and Humpback Mountains in central Virginia; near Compton Gap in Shenandoah National Park; between Milesburn Road and Sandy Sod in Pennsylvania; north of Eph's Lookout in Massachusetts; near Pinkham Notch and in the Carter–Moriah Range in New Hampshire; and north of East B. Hill Road and north of ME 27 in Maine.

GAYWINGS

Polygala paucifolia

FLOWER:
   *A most delicate plant, Gaywings'
flowers grow on a long stem from the
upper leaf axils. Two purplish-pink
lateral sepals form flaring wings
while the petals form a tube with a
fringed, yellow, or pink crest.*

BLOOM SEASON:
   May to June

LEAVES AND STEM:
   *Only three to six inches high, the
plant has broad evergreen leaves that
are crowded near the top of the stem,
but smaller and more scalelike lower
down.*

RANGE:
   Georgia to Maine

Sometimes mistaken as an orchid or a part of the Pea family, the Gaywings are actually a member of the Milkwort family. The Milkworts received their common name from the once-held belief that the plants could stimulate and increase the amount of milk that cows and nursing mothers could produce. The Gaywings' genus and species names also reflect this belief; the two Greek words *poly* and *gala*, when joined together, translate into "much milk." Interestingly, the word *gala* also served as the basis for the English word for what we call the Milky Way—a galaxy.

Like all flowers, there is a reason why Gaywings, also known as Fringed Polygala, grow in the form in which they do. When insects land upon the protruding pouch, their weight pushes it down, enabling the sex organs to pop through a small cleft at the top of the pouch and deposit pollen on the insect's body. The flower's interesting structure has resulted in some quite inventive descriptions. It has been likened to a tiny tailless airplane, a bird on the wing, an awakening butterfly, and a dragonfly.

Like Jewelweed (*Impatiens capensis;* see page 114), Gaywings also produce what are known as cleistogamous flowers. You will probably have to get down on hands and knees and inspect the plant where it emerges from the ground to find them. Growing from small branchlets, the cleistogamous flowers never really open, but do self-fertilize themselves, thereby insuring the propagation of the plant— if for some reason the main flower fails to become fertilized.

Some places along the AT you are likely to encounter Gaywings: Between Bluff Mountain and Hot Springs, and between High Rocks and Spivey Gap in North Carolina; north and south of VA 624, close to Jennings Creek, on Fork Mountain, and in the James River Face Wilderness in central Virginia.

CATAWBA RHODODENDRON

Rhododendron catawbiensis

FLOWER:
Making one of the most colorful displays, the light pink to dark pink to rich purple flowers are about two inches across, are open bell-shaped, have five lobes, and grow in large and ornate clusters.

BLOOM SEASON:
May to June

LEAVES AND STEM:
The distinctive, oblong, shiny, leathery, evergreen leaves, three to five inches long, grow on shrubs that usually range from four to ten feet in height.

RANGE:
Georgia to northern Virginia

If there are any two plants that define the beauty, abundance, and impressive array of wildflowers found along the AT, especially the southern portion of the pathway, they would have to include the Mountain Laurel (*Kalmia latifolia;* see page 146) and the Rhododendron. Both grow in thickets so dense they can nearly cover entire mountainsides, and indeed they do blanket the summits of numerous mountains in Georgia, North Carolina, and Tennessee.

Blooming in late May, along with, or just after, one of its relatives, the Pink Azalea (*Rhododendron nudiflorum;* see page 130), Catawba Rhododendron's pink to deep purple clusters of flowers are so lush and awe inspiring that they have attracted people from around the world. Hikers trek well over two miles (from the nearest roadway) across the high country of the Mount Rogers area in southwest Virginia just to be able to enjoy the display of flowers spreading out along the ridgeline in Rhododendron Gap. A few weeks later, on the higher elevations along the North Carolina–Tennessee border, 1,200 acres of Catawba Rhododendrons bloom in a natural garden on the summit of Roan Mountain. This impressive event is celebrated by a festival that has been held each year for many decades now.

Catawba Rhododendron reaches its northern limits somewhere around Shenandoah National Park, yet the Great Rhododendron (*Rhododendron maximum;* see page 199) can be found in some isolated spots all of the way into New England. Its clusters of white flowers appear in time to grow alongside those of the Mountain Laurel.

Some places along the AT you are likely to encounter one of the Rhododendrons: Along Stover Creek in Georgia; at Muskrat Creek Shelter, near Albert Mountain, and on Wayah Bald in North Carolina; at Bearwallow Gap along the North Carolina–Tennessee border; in Laurel Fork Gorge in Tennessee; and next to Thunder Hill Shelter in central Virginia.

MOUNTAIN LAUREL

Kalmia latifolia

FLOWER:

Growing in clusters, the nearly one-inch, cup-shaped flowers vary from pink to white. Radiating from the center, the flower's ten stamens create a distinctive spoke design.

BLOOM SEASON:

May to July

LEAVES AND STEM:

The shrub usually grows from five to ten feet in height, but can, on rare occasions, reach as high as thirty-five feet. The evergreen leaves are sometimes confused with Rhododendron leaves, but are smaller and more slender.

RANGE:

Georgia to portions of New England

Take a look at the individual blossoms of the Mountain Laurel and you will find a most ingenious pollination mechanism. The five petals (each with two small notches) are connected together to form a shallow bowl. The ten stamens growing from the center of the petals are tucked inside the notches. A single pistil rises to the outside of the petals. When an insect visitor (usually a bee) arrives to gather nectar, it brushes against the bent over stamens. This moves them around enough to cause their tops to break free of the notches, spring upward, and toss pollen from the anthers onto the insect's body. Moving on to the next flower, the insect can't help but brush against its pistil, thereby depositing the pollen and ensuring fertilization.

In addition to the usual way plants propagate themselves, Mountain Laurel reproduces by sending up new shoots from its spreading root system, or, when branches touch the ground, by growing new roots, which radiate outward and, in turn, send up shoots of their own. This is how Mountain Laurel is able to develop into the dense thickets that you see.

If you are hiking in the fall, stop to examine the small capsules on the Mountain Laurel; these were once the plant's flowers in June and July. Break one open and you will see what appears to be a brown powder. Each speck of dust is actually a seed of the Mountain Laurel—a seed so small that it would take thousands of them just to fill a tiny thimble.

Some places along the AT you are likely to encounter Mountain Laurel: On Blood Mountain and near Bull Gap in Georgia; on Little Rock Knob on the North Carolina–Tennessee border; in Laurel Fork Gorge in Tennessee; throughout Michaux State Forest in Pennsylvania; on the lower slopes of Lions Head and Bear Mountain in Connecticut; near Benedict Pond and upon the north slope of Race Mountain in Massachusetts.

DEPTFORD PINK

Dianthus armeria

FLOWER:
The beautifully pink, half-inch-in-diameter flowers are speckled with white dots. They have five cut-edged petals with ten stamens, and they grow in small clusters on the top of firm, upright stems.

BLOOM SEASON:
May to July

LEAVES AND STEM:
The lower leaves are opposite, narrow, and one to four inches long. Just below the flowers are small, upright, light green bracts.

RANGE:
Georgia to Maine

A European import that escaped from the early settler's gardens, Deptford Pink is now such a common flower that—in addition to being found along the length of the trail—it inhabits fields, roadsides, and wasteplaces as far north as Ontario and Quebec and as far west as Missouri.

The flower was named for Deptford, England, an administrative district of London where it once covered vast meadows with its lovely pink color. The area is now industrialized, and the Deptford Pink hangs on by growing in small fields and along heavily traveled roadways.

The generic name, *Dianthus*, is derived from a coupling of the word *dios*—referring to the Greek god Zeus—with the word *anthos*—for flower. Thus, translated, the name means "divine flower" or "God's flower."

A relative, Maiden Pink (*Dianthus deltoides*), only ranges from about New Jersey to Vermont along the AT. It can be distinguished from Deptford Pink by its larger flowers, whose petals are more rounded and heavily toothed. Its flowers also grow solitarily on a stem instead of in small clusters.

The genus *Dianthus* includes the commercially grown Carnations, popular in bouquets and corsages. The history of these flowers goes as far back as an early Christian tale. According to the story, Carnations grew from the fallen tears that Mary shed when she saw Jesus struggling to carry the cross.

Some places along the AT you are likely to encounter Deptford Pink: Several trail crossings of the Blue Ridge Parkway and Bryant Ridge in central Virginia; and between Gifford Woods State Park and River Road in Vermont.

INDIAN PAINTBRUSH

Castilleja coccinea

FLOWER:
   On a plant whose leaf bracts are its most colorful attribute, the one-inch-long, greenish yellow flowers are easy to overlook. The tubular blossoms are made up of a two-lobed upper lip folding over a three-lobed lower one.

BLOOM SEASON:
   May to July

LEAVES AND STEM:
   The basal leaves grow in rosettes and are one to three inches long. Rising on a one- to two-foot stem, the upper, fan-shaped leaf bracts are, by far, the most conspicuous part of the plant as they are tipped in deep scarlet.

RANGE:
   Georgia to Massachusetts (with isolated plants having been found in southern Maine)

Those who have strolled through the sagebrush country, open grasslands, or alpine meadows of the western portion of North America may be surprised to find a familiar looking plant while hiking along the AT. However, the flowers of the Indian Paintbrush will probably not be the first things to catch your eye when you come upon it in open fields, sandy soil, meadows, or along woodland borders. There is no doubt that your gaze will be drawn to the upper leaf bracts, which are tipped in the deep scarlet color of some of the best sunsets you may have been privileged to witness while hiking.

It is sunsets, in fact, which gave rise to the plant's common name. According to a Native American legend, an Indian brave trying to paint a picture of the evening sky became disconcerted because his collection of dyes could not do justice to the atmospheric display he was witnessing. In answer to his prayers, the Great Spirit sent him paintbrushes wet with the most vibrant hues he had ever seen. When the brave finished his painting, he tossed the brushes aside, and wherever one landed, an Indian Paintbrush plant began to grow.

Following the Doctrine of Signatures, Indian Paintbrush has been used as a balm for burned skin, the redness that results from the sting of a centipede, and as a treatment for venereal diseases. Native American women also made a drink from the plant to help control their menstrual flow.

Some places along the AT you are likely to encounter Indian Paintbrush: Just east of Woody Gap in Georgia.

GOAT'S RUE

Tephrosia virginiana

FLOWER:
 Growing in clusters at and near the top of the stem, the three-quarter-inch flowers have a yellowish upper petal and lower pink wings.

BLOOM SEASON:
 May to August

LEAVES AND STEM:
 The compound leaves are pinnately divided into oblong leaflets on a silvery stem one to two feet in height.

RANGE:
 Georgia to Vermont/New Hampshire

Observant northbound AT thru-hikers will notice that Goat's Rue is a companion of theirs for much of their journey—as the plant ranges from Georgia to central New England and is in bloom from May well into August.

For such a common plant, Goat's Rue has an exceedingly pretty and showy flower, which can range in color from bright yellow and pink to a deep gold and rich purple. With a disposition toward dry woodlands, open fields, thickets, and roadsides with sandy soils, it was once fed to goats in order to increase their production of milk. That practice has since been discontinued, since it is now known that the plant contains the substance retenone, a poison used in commercially produced insecticides. However, certain birds, including wild turkeys, do feed upon the plant's seeds, and Native Americans used Goat's Rue as a cough medicine and as a treatment for worms and bladder problems.

Goat's Rue is a member of the Pea family. This huge kinship includes peas, lentils, beans, soybeans, peanuts, clovers, alfalfas, vetches, sensitive plants, wild indigoes, tick trefoils, wisterias, and kudzu. Even some trees which grow along the AT are members of the Pea family. Among them are redbud, yellowwood, and black locust. Almost every constituent of the family produces a fruit that closely resembles a pea or bean pod, with seeds growing in a row inside one chamber that can be accessed through one or two narrow seams.

Some places along the AT you are likely to encounter Goat's Rue: At Black Horse Gap and south of Highcock Knob in central Virginia; and several of the dirt road crossings of the Long Trail in Vermont.

SHEEP LAUREL

Kalmia angustifolia

FLOWER:
 The half-inch-wide, rich pink flowers have five petals and are arranged in lush clusters around the stem.

BLOOM SEASON:
 May to August

LEAVES AND STEM:
 The two-inch-long, evergreen leaves have a paler underside and grow in whorls of three.

RANGE:
 Georgia to Maine

Like its relative, Mountain Laurel (*Kalmia latifolia;* see page 146), the flowers of the Sheep Laurel have five petals connected together to form a shallow bowl. The ten stamens growing from the center of the petals are tucked inside notches on the petals. When brushed by a bee or butterfly, the stamens spring upward, sending a cascade of pollen onto the visiting insect.

Although they are similar in appearance, Mountain Laurel flowers grow in terminal clusters, while those of the Sheep Laurel are smaller in size and are arranged around the stem—most often below newer, upright, terminal leaves.

The Laurels received their genus name in honor of Pehr Kalm, a Swede who roamed the eastern portion of North America in the mid-1700s collecting unknown species. A pupil of the famous botanist Linneaus, Kalm returned to Europe with more than six hundred specimens. As he was classifying these plants, Linneaus named the Laurels after Kalm in recognition of his student's labors.

Sheep Laurel is sometimes commonly referred to as Lambkill because it is highly poisonous to grazing livestock.

A relative, Pale Laurel (*Kalmia polifolia*), has a range as far south as New Jersey and Pennsylvania but is only seen in great numbers around the boggy areas of New England. Its pink flowers, which grow in terminal clusters above leaves that grow in pairs, are rolled along the edges and are very white on the undersides. The small twigs of this plant have two noticeable edges.

Some places along the AT you are likely to encounter Sheep Laurel: At Pig Farm Campsite in central Virginia; north of Eph's Lookout in Massachusetts; on and around White Rocks Cliff in Vermont; around Ethan Pond in New Hampshire; and in the Barren–Chairback Range and along Cooper Brook in Maine.

MOUNTAIN CRANBERRY

Vaccinium vitis-idaea

FLOWER:
The quarter-inch, pink, nodding flowers are bell-shaped with the four lobes slightly bending backwards.

BLOOM SEASON:
June to July

LEAVES AND STEM:
Growing on creeping stems with branches three to seven inches in height, the tough, shiny, evergreen leaves are less than one inch in length and have black spots underneath.

RANGE:
Found almost exclusively in northern New England.

Mountain Cranberry, whose other common names include Lingonberry and Lowbush Cranberry, is a member of the Heath family. This family is one of the most commonly found along the AT, so that at least one of its members, which include Trailing Arbutus (*Epigaea repens;* see page 12) and Wintergreen (*Gaultheria procumbens;* see page 92), can be found anywhere along length of the AT. Another member, the diminutive Alpine Azalea (*Loiseleuria procumbens;* see page 199) clings to the higher elevations of Maine and New Hampshire.

The Mountain Cranberry's flowers develop from the previous year's buds and grow in groups of up to fifteen on terminal racemes. The flowers, in turn, develop into rich, dark red berries in late summer, adding a touch of color to the rocky mountain slopes or wet boggy areas on which they grow. The newly formed fruits can be quite bitter, but those that have stayed on the plant over the winter can be a sweet, tasty treat for hikers who are trekking across the mountains in northern New Hampshire and Maine in the early spring. Humans are not the only ones to enjoy the berries. Snowshoe hares, bears, and moose all browse on the fruit, while red foxes and red-backed voles consume mass quantities. Many migrating birds obtain sustenance from the berries as they head northward in the spring.

The tough, evergreen leaves and hardy stems of the plant are able to resist desiccation and damage by high winds and ice storms. The plant contains the substance arbutin, which is used by pharmaceutical companies in the production of medications to treat intestinal disorders.

Some places along the AT you are likely to encounter Mountain Cranberry: On Kinsman Ridge, on Mount Lafayette, between Zealand Falls Hut and Ethan Pond, and on Mount Pierce and Mount Clinton in New Hampshire; and along the ridges and summits of Saddleback, The Horn, and Saddleback Jr. in Maine.

Sundew

Drosera rotundifolia

FLOWER:

The small (a quarter-inch across) flowers have five petals (with a pink coloration), five sepals, five stamens, and a pistil. They grow in a one-sided cluster along a stem, four to nine inches in height, and they usually open one at a time.

BLOOM SEASON:

June to August

LEAVES AND STEM:

The small round leaves, no more than three-quarters of an inch in size, grow in a rosette around the main flower stem. Each leaf is on its own hairy, thin, half-inch stalk and is covered in reddish-colored, glandular hairs which secrete a sweet, sticky substance.

RANGE:

Georgia to Maine

Some of the most interesting of the plants found along the AT are the carnivorous ones. As school children, we were all fascinated by the Venus's-Flytrap, but there are more than 450 species of carnivorous plants worldwide, many of them growing in water-saturated habitats, dry rocky areas, or similarly nutrient-impoverished environments. To compensate for the meager nourishment they obtain from the soil, these plants have developed the capability of digesting insects and other small animals to obtain essential nitrogen, phosphorus, vitamins, and other trace minerals.

Believed to have near-tropical origins, Sundews have a burst of growth during the heat of midsummer, usually rising above the surrounding hummocks of sphagnum mosses. Its glandular hairs, coated with a glistening, sweet, sticky fluid on rosettes of small leaves, attract insects, which then become entangled in some of the longer outer hairs. In a unique occurrence, the hairs begin a growth spurt, adding cells that enable them to "fold" over the insect and draw it into more intimate contact with the leaf, where shorter hairs secrete digestive enzymes. If the prey is quite active, the hairs respond quickly and can encircle the victim in less than twenty minutes. If the prey is already dead, the plant seems to recognize that there is no urgent need to ensnare it, and the plant may take several days to complete the process.

Some places along the AT you are likely to encounter Sundew: Near the stream at Zealand Falls Hut and in the alpine bog on Mount Jackson in New Hampshire; and in Fourth Mountain Bog in Maine.

PURPLE-FLOWERING
RASPBERRY

Rubus odoratus

FLOWER:
The one- to two-inch, lavender flowers have five roselike petals and numerous stamens and pistils. The flowers are more of a deep rose color than they are purple.

BLOOM SEASON:
June to August

LEAVES AND STEM:
The maple-shaped leaves are four to ten inches in width and grow on reddish brown stems that are both hairy and sticky. Purple-flowering Raspberry is a bush that can attain heights of well over five feet.

RANGE:
Georgia to Maine

Of all of the raspberry bushes along the trail, visitors to the AT are most likely to encounter the Purple-Flowering Raspberry. Sadly, its berries—although edible—are not very appetizing. They may look appealing on the plant, but they are dry, pithy, acidic, and—according to one thru-hiker's entry written in a trailside shelter register—"quite insipid in taste."

It may not be good to eat, but this fruit is worthy of closer study. Unlike many fruits that are one solid piece, raspberries are made up of numerous small, separate sections. Protruding from each of these sections is a tiny hair—a remnant of what was once one of the many pistils of the flower from which the fruit developed!

The stems of the Raspberry plant grow in two-year cycles. In the first year, the roots send up long, straight stems that produce leaves, but no branches or flowers. In the second year, the stems grow side branches on which the flowers and fruits grow. After this, the main stems die back; the roots send up new stems the following year.

Native Americans, especially the Cherokees that lived in the Great Smoky Mountains through which the AT now passes, used the Purple-Flowering Raspberry for a number of purposes. A pleasant tasting tea was made from the plant to alleviate a toothache, while the astringent liquid was used to cleanse open sores and wounds. Chewing on Raspberry roots would help stop painful coughing.

Some places along the AT you are likely to encounter Purple-Flowering Raspberry: South of Sawtooth Ridge in central Virginia; and close to Piazza Rock, and near East Flagstaff Road in Maine.

HOLLOW
JOE-PYE WEED

Eupatorium fistulosum

FLOWER:
   The tubular, fuzzy, pink to purple flowers grow in a dome-shaped cluster on the end of a stem two to eight feet high.

BLOOM SEASON:
   July to September

LEAVES AND STEM:
   The lanceolate leaves, four to twelve inches long, are roughly toothed and grow in whorls along the hollow stem. Most often the whorls consist of six leaves, but they may number anywhere from four to seven.

RANGE:
   Georgia to Maine

Hollow Joe-Pye Weed is named after a Native American herbalist who supposedly roamed the New England countryside in the late 1700s. Using parts of the plant (mixed with liquor), he treated the locals for a variety of ailments. Although the story seems to be based more on legend than on fact, there is a tavern in Massachusetts whose ledgers show that a Joe-Pye purchased rum there in the 1770s.

The genus name *Eupatorium* has an even more colorful origin. Eupator was the emperor of Pontus, a kingdom in Asia Minor during the first century B.C. He is believed to be the first person to use plants of this genus for medicinal purposes. Like many rulers, Eupator was concerned about being removed from power. Discovering that the plants were an antidote to poison, he consumed large quantities of them. When his enemies finally imprisoned him, he tried to poison himself, but being so full of the antidote, he finally had to resort to having a servant stab him to death.

A flower most often associated with the heat of late summer, there are a number of different species of Joe-Pye Weed that may be found along the AT. Spotted Joe-Pye Weed (*Eupatorium maculatum*) ranges from Georgia to Maine and has a deep purple or purple spotted stem. Joe-Pye Weed (*Eupatorium dubium*) has about the same range and appearance, but it is a smaller plant whose leaves are more rounded. Sweet Joe-Pye Weed (*Eupatorium purpureum*) may be found from Georgia to New Hampshire and has a greenish stem with bits of purple and black near the leaf joints.

Some places along the AT you are likely to encounter one of the Joe-Pye Weeds: Between Beech Gap and Big Spring Shelter in North Carolina; on Peters Mountain, Cold Mountain, Tar Jacket Ridge, and Humpback Mountain in central Virginia; at many of the trail crossings of Skyline Drive in Shenandoah National Park; at Benedict Pond and in the Hop Brook floodplain in Massachusetts; and north of the Kennebec River in Maine.

BEE BALM

Monarda didyma

FLOWER:
    The individual bright red flowers of the Bee Balm are about one-and-a-half inches long and have an ascending upper lip with a broader, drooping lower lip. Although most books typically say the flowers grow in a dense terminal cluster, Roger Tory Peterson refers to it as a "ragged scarlet pompon of tubular flowers."

BLOOM SEASON:
    July to September

LEAVES AND STEM:
    The three- to six-inch, dark green leaves are quite toothed and grow in pairs along the length of the two- to four-foot stem.

RANGE:
    Georgia to New Jersey/New York

Bee Balm is a member of the Mint family, and as such, it has been used as a scent in perfumes and as a flavoring in cooking. Its leaves and early shoots have been added to salads, drinks, and even jellies. While studying the flower, you may notice that its stem is different from those of most other plants. Run your fingers up and down and you will find that the stem is not round, but square, a characteristic it shares with other members of the Mint family.

Growing in moist woods and along small streams, colonies of Bee Balm are conspicuous in the forest; their three- to four-foot-tall stems, which tower above other undergrowth, are topped by tubular flowers of the deepest, richest scarlet to be found on any wildflower.

Although bees are attracted to the flower, the long floral tubes, which make it hard for most insects to reach the nectar, are more suited to the bills of hummingbirds, which are attracted by the blossom's brilliant red.

As part of a group negotiating a treaty in 1743 with the Oswego Indians of New York, naturalist John Bartram learned that the Native Americans made a tea from Bee Balm that helped alleviate the discomforts of fevers or chills. The drink soon became popular with colonists who used it as a substitute for imported tea, and earned the plant one of its other common names, Oswego Tea. Based upon the Doctrine of Signatures, the red flowers were once believed to be able to cleanse blood of any impurities.

Some places along the AT you are likely to encounter Bee Balm: Around Cosby Knob Shelter in Great Smoky Mountains National Park, between Little Laurel Shelter and Jerry Cabin Shelter, and between Grassy Ridge and Hump Mountain on the North Carolina–Tennessee border; along Brown Mountain Creek in central Virginia; and across the footbridge leading from the AT to Fuller Lake Beach in Pine Grove Furnace State Park in Pennsylvania.

CARDINAL FLOWER

Lobelia cardinalis

FLOWER:

The brilliant red flowers grow in a long cluster, are about one-and-a-half inches long, and have five petals that form two lips; the upper lip has two lobes, while the lower one has three spreading lobes. The stamens are united in a tube around the single pistil.

BLOOM SEASON:

July to September

LEAVES AND STEM:

The lanceolate leaves average six inches in length, are irregularly toothed, and grow alternately on a stem two to five feet in height.

RANGE:

Georgia to Maine

A brilliant red flower, Roger Tory Peterson once described the Cardinal Flower as America's favorite. In their book *Southern Wild Flowers and Trees* published in 1901, Alice Lounsberry and Mrs. Ellis Brown were so taken by the flower that they wrote, "Cardinal Flower is a wild flower about which the nation might feel a righteous pride, so intensely coloured and velvety in texture . . . defying the artist's pigments to imitate them, and forming against their background of dark green and lustrous leaves a wild bit of colour almost without equal. Old men, urchins and little maids all seek it by the brook's side."

Found in the same type of habitat as Bee Balm (*Monarda didyma;* see page 164)—in moist areas and along water runs—the plant is named not for the state bird of Virginia and West Virginia, but rather for the color of vestments worn by Cardinals of the Roman Catholic Church. The genus name of *Lobelia* honors a Flemish herbalist who was the personal physician of James I of England.

Hummingbirds are the plant's main pollinators, as their bills are perfectly suited to reach the nectar located at the end of the flower tube, which is too narrow and too long for most insects. In addition to propagating itself by seeds, the Cardinal Flower can send out little shoots that rise above the ground as a small cluster of leaves. The following year the small shoots develop into mature flowering plants and send out their own shoots. This is why, when you are lucky enough to find one, you will probably find a whole colony of the flowers.

Some places along the AT you are likely to encounter Cardinal Flower: Near Laurel Falls in Tennessee; on the south side of Poor Valley in southwest Virginia; in Johns Hollow in central Virginia; in Pine Grove Furnace State Park in Pennsylvania; and near Bulls Bridge and north of Stony Brook in Connecticut.

CRESTED DWARF IRIS

Iris cristata

FLOWER:

The pale to deep purple flowers are divided into six parts. The three petals are narrow and arching, while the three petal-like sepals are broader, curve downward, are streaked with purple, and are "crested" with white to yellow ridges.

BLOOM SEASON:

April to May

LEAVES AND STEM:

The lanceolate leaves are one-half to one inch wide. They sheath the three- to eight-inch stem and may grow to twelve inches in length.

RANGE:

Georgia to Maryland

Blooming about the same time as Mayapple (*Podophyllum peltatum;* see page 26), the Crested Dwarf Iris, as well as its Iris relatives, was named by the Greeks for their goddess of the rainbow. Iris was the messenger of Juno—the protectress of women—and the rainbow was the bridge she utilized for her frequent errands between the heavens and earth. One of her duties was to lead the souls of women to the Elysian Fields; for this reason the Greeks would put Irises on the graves of their mothers, wives, and sisters.

When Louis VII adopted the Iris as the emblem of his house, it became known as the *fleur-de-lis,* the "Flower of Louis," and it was used as a symbol of France's victory in the Second Crusade.

In many ways *Iris cristata*, which appears to prefer wooded slopes and ravines, resembles its larger domesticated relative, *Iris germanica,* and a number of other Irises. The Dwarf Iris (*Iris verna*) shares almost the same range but does not have the white to yellow ridge on the outer segments of the flower. Its leaves are narrower and more grasslike. The Slender Blue-Flag Iris (*Iris prismatica*), which ranges from Georgia to Virginia along the AT, has light blue flowers with three sepals containing a yellowish spot at their base, all growing on a stem one to two feet in height. Bigger and wider, Larger Blue-Flag Iris (*Iris versicolor*) is found in marshy areas and wet meadows from Virginia to Maine.

Some places along the AT you are likely to encounter one of the Irises: Between Springer Mountain and Neel's Gap in Georgia; between Boy Scout Shelter and Catawba Shelter, near Bear Wallow Gap, and in James River Face Wilderness in central Virginia; in Michaux State Forest in Pennsylvania; throughout the Housatonic Valley in Connecticut; and around Ethyl Pond in Maine.

WILD GINGER

Asarum canadense

FLOWER:

Wild Ginger's one-inch, brownish, cup-shaped flower (which gave rise to one of its other common names, Little Brown Jug) has three pointed and spreading lobes, twelve stamens, and one six-lobed pistil. It grows almost at ground level on a short stalk in the crotch of two leaves.

BLOOM SEASON:

April to May

LEAVES AND STEM:

The pair of heart-shaped, hairy leaves span about three inches in width and grow on stalks of up to twelve inches in height.

RANGE:

Georgia to Maine

Not one of the most attractive wildflowers found along the trail, Wild Ginger is, nonetheless, certainly one of the most interesting. The flower is often overlooked by AT hikers because its color closely approximates that of the soil around it. It may also be hidden by its own foliage, as it rises no more than a couple of inches from the ground.

There are a number of reasons why the flower has evolved into its particular color, shape, and size. Blooming in the early spring, the low-growing blossoms are some of the first to be located by small flies and gnats as they emerge from the ground in search of sustenance. Being carrion eaters, these insects are attracted by the flower's purplish-brown, rotting-flesh color. Once inside the jug-shaped flower, they can feast on the abundant pollen—protected from the chilly winds of springtime.

Wild Ginger is not related to the ginger you purchase in the supermarket to add to Asian dishes. Yet, its rhizome tastes similar and has been used as a substitute. Early settlers made a sweet treat by cutting up the rootstocks and cooking them for several days in a syrupy, sugar water. The candied roots would keep for long periods of time and could be carried into the field to provide a refreshing snack. Native Americans used ground Wild Ginger root to help preserve meats, and a member of the Lewis and Clark expedition had an open wound treated with a concoction containing bits of the ground-up root. Not surprisingly, modern medicine has discovered that the plant has an ingredient that is effective in treating bacterial infections.

Some places along the AT you are likely to encounter Wild Ginger: From Jennings Creek to north of Bryant Ridge Shelter in central Virginia; in Caledonia State Park in Pennsylvania; along the trail above the Housatonic River in Connecticut; and in the hardwood forest west of Kent Pond in Vermont.

BLUETS

Houstonia caerulea

FLOWER:
Four, light blue to almost white petals are joined together with a slightly yellow center. Each stem has a solitary flower.

BLOOM SEASON:
April to late June and early July

LEAVES AND STEM:
Leaves are opposite and mostly basal on a two- to eight-inch stem.

RANGE:
Georgia to Maine

Although northbound AT thru-hikers become acquainted with the tiny Bluet as it lines the trail in large mats along the North Carolina–Tennessee border, the flower grows well throughout the length of the AT. The genus and species name is Latin for "sky blue," an obviously descriptive name for the petals. The flowers, with their delicately upturned petals, reflect the cleanliness and clarity of an unclouded sky, which may account for another common name—Quaker-Lady.

Some sources say that the species *caerulea* appears in two different colors and forms. On one form, the stamens (with their anthers full of pollen) huddle down in the flower, while the pistils (which are designed to catch the pollen) stick out. In the other form of the flower, the opposite is true. In order to produce seeds, each type usually must obtain pollen from its own kind (but not from its same colony). Known as dimorphism, this scheme of two different types of flowers is believed to create seeds that are hardier and more likely to sprout.

Favoring deciduous forests, grassy hillsides, and open fields, a number of related species of Bluets can be found along the AT. Ranging from Georgia to Maine, Long-Leaved Bluets (*Houstonia longifolia*) have terminal clusters of two to three, white to pale purple flowers. Found no further north than Pennsylvania and New Jersey, Large or Mountain Houstonia (*Houstonia purpurea;* see page 190) has ribbed leaves that grow oppositely on a four- to eighteen-inch stem and white or pink flowers that grow in terminal clusters.

Some places along the AT you are likely to encounter one of the Bluets: Between Springer Mountain and Neels Gap in Georgia; between Deep Gap and Wallace Gap in North Carolina; on the mountains along the North Carolina–Tennessee border; near Tinker Cliffs and along Humpback Mountain in central Virginia; in the open areas of Lions Head in Connecticut; along the Long Trail in Vermont; and near Stratton Brook in Maine.

SPIDERWORT

Tradescantia virginiana

FLOWER:

The violet flowers grow in a terminal cluster, each having three rounded petals, from which spring six hairy stamens of yellowish gold.

BLOOM SEASON:

April to July

LEAVES AND STEM:

The fifteen-inch, irislike leaves are folded lengthwise and grow oppositely on a stem one to two feet high.

RANGE:

Georgia to Maine (but increasingly rarer north of Connecticut)

If you stay at the same site for a couple of days, camped beside some nearby Spiderwort plants, the flowers you enjoy on the first morning will not be the same ones that grace your presence the next day. After pollination, each blossom lasts but a day, only to be replaced by a new one that unfolds the following morning. This process is so unlike other flowers, which just shrivel up and fall off, that it behooves you to observe the Spiderwort during the course of the day. Closing by midday, the enzyme action in the fertilized flowers causes them to turn into runny, gelatinous blobs.

The plant has some other interesting properties. Scientists have discovered that a thin, mucilaginous thread can be pulled from the jointed stems; the thread quickly hardens when exposed to the air. Researchers have also found that the plant can detect lower levels of radiation than ordinary electronic equipment. Within two weeks of exposure, cells in the Spiderwort mutate and cause the blossoms, especially the hairy stamens, to change from violet-blue to bright pink. The higher the level of radiation, the higher the number of cells that mutate. Because the plant responds in similar ways to other types of pollution (such as high levels of pesticides or carbon monoxide), it is now commercially grown and replanted at specific sites as a monitoring tool.

Another Spiderwort that may be spotted along the trail is Zigzag Spiderwort (*Tradescantia subaspera*), which ranges from Georgia to Virginia and has a zigzagging stem with blue flowers. Ohio Spiderwort (*Tradescantia ohiensis*), found from Georgia to Massachusetts, has flowers ranging from blue to light red.

Some places along the AT you are likely to encounter one of the Spiderworts: On the south side of Wesser Bald in North Carolina; between Little Laurel Shelter and Jerry Cabin Shelter along the North Carolina–Tennessee border; and south of Tinker Cliffs, along Thunder Hill, and on Humpback Mountain in central Virginia.

GRAY BEARDTONGUE

Penstemon canescens

FLOWER:
The Gray Beardtongue's tubular-shaped flowers are about one inch long and have two lips. The lower lip has three lobes which project straight out, while the upper one—with two lobes—stands erect. The lower lip is streaked by dark purple lines.

BLOOM SEASON:
May to July

LEAVES AND STEM:
The lanceolate leaves are two to six inches long. The upper ones tend to clasp the stem, which ranges from one to three feet in height. The basal leaves are broader and have stalks.

RANGE:
Georgia to Pennsylvania

Beardtongues are members of the Snapdragon family, which includes Butter-and-Eggs (*Linaria vulgaris;* see page 118), Indian Paintbrush (*Castilleja coccinea;* see page 150), the False Foxgloves (*Aureolaria spp.;* see page 199), and Lousewort (*Pedicularis canadensis;* see page 96). Gray Beardtongue tends to favor dry woods and rocky slopes, while other members of the genus enjoy the sunshine along roadsides and in open meadows. Roger Tory Peterson claims that there are well over a dozen different Beardtongues that may be found in the eastern part of the United States and that even experts have trouble identifying the individual species.

In addition to finding Gray Beardtongue along the trail, it is possible you may come across Hairy Beardtongue (*Penstemon hirsutus*), which ranges from Georgia to Maine and has pink to pale purple flowers along with a downy stem, one to three feet high. Smooth Beardtongue (*Penstemon laevigatus*) grows from Georgia to Pennsylvania New Jersey and has a stem that lacks hairs along its entire length, except just below the flower cluster. Its leaves have nearly inconspicuous tooths above the midpoint. Foxglove Beardtongue (*Penstemon digitalis*) ranges from Georgia to Maine, reaches a height close to four feet, sometimes has pinkish flowers, and may be the most widespread of the Beardtongues in the eastern United States.

All of the Beardtongues are named for one of the five stamens that lacks an anther. These sexless anthers have a tuft of hair hanging down like a beard. The plants are often commonly referred to by their genus name, *Penstemon*, which translates to mean "five stamens." Native Americans found the Beardtongues to be useful in treating venereal diseases.

Some places along the AT you are likely to encounter one of the Beardtongues: On the north side of Blood Mountain in Georgia; along the Nolichucky River in Tennessee; and less than one mile north of Boy Scout Shelter in central Virginia.

PITCHER PLANT

Sarracenia purpurea

The Pitcher Plant, found most easily along the AT in the Fourth Mountain Bog along Maine's Barren-Chairback Range, has red-veined vase- or pitcher-shaped leaves that contain water and enzymes in the bottom. These leaves are perfectly designed to entice and capture. A sweet substance secreted by nectar glands on the leaf's edges attracts insects, while downward-pointing hairs entice them to descend further into the plant but make climbing back out nearly impossible. The inside of the leaf contains easily dislodged sticky cells that adhere to the prey's feet, further decreasing mobility. Exhausted, the prey slides down to the pool of liquid where digestive enzymes and bacteria break down the insect's body—so that the plant can easily absorb it through the porous walls of the pitcher.

Amazingly, there are some insects that make their homes in or on the Pitcher Plant. A certain species of mosquito lives in the plant's liquid and may even overwinter there when it becomes encased in ice. The larva of one species of fly survives by eating the remains of other insects that fall into the plant, while a small wasp builds its nest inside the pitcher. Spiders have learned to spin webs across the mouth of the pitcher to capture insects attracted to the smell of the plant, and tree frogs have been seen enjoying tasty insect meals while sitting on the lip of the pitcher. However, some frogs have paid a dear price for this easy hunting stand—they have fallen into the pitcher and have become a large meal for the plant.

Some places along the AT you are likely to encounter Pitcher Plants: In the bog areas around Ethan Pond in New Hampshire; and in the Fourth Mountain Bog and other bogs in the 100-mile wilderness, and along the shores of Crescent Pond in Maine.

VIPER'S BUGLOSS

Echium vulgare

FLOWER:

The showy, bluish flowers are about one inch long and have noticeably protruding red stamens and an upper lip that is longer than the lower one.

BLOOM SEASON:

June to September

LEAVES AND STEM:

The alternate, two- to six-inch, lanceolate leaves are sessile on the stem; the plant usually rises about one to three feet from the ground.

RANGE:

Georgia to Maine

Viper's Bugloss was imported from Europe in the late seventeenth century and has now spread to the point that it can be found in every one of the AT states. A common plant, it produces a colorful flower. When they first appear, the buds display an often pleasing shade of pink. Spreading outward, the petals become a vivid purplish blue, accented by long stamens of a rich red hue. The petals may change color again, becoming reddish purple with age.

The plant appears to prefer limestone and gravelly soils and is most often found in old fields, wasteplaces, along roadsides, and in sunny meadows through which the trail passes. It received the first part of its common name because some people imagined its seed looked like the head of a snake. (Some sources say it was given the name because the plant was believed to be a remedy for snake bites.) The bugloss part of the name is from old Greek and means "ox-tongue," which the leaves supposedly resemble.

Viper's Bugloss is a member of the Forget-Me-Not family, which contains close to 100 genera and 2,000 species worldwide. Characteristic of the family, the plant's flowers are arranged in a one-sided coil that gradually unfolds as it grows. (This is reminiscent of the way that the tightly wound fiddleheads of a fern plant open up to become spreading leaf fronds.)

Some references point out that you should wash your hand immediately after touching the plant, as the hairy bristles protruding from the leaves can cause skin irritations.

Some places along the AT you are likely to encounter Viper's Bugloss: Near Doll Flats along the North Carolina–Tennessee border; at Pig Farm Campsite, Tar Jacket Ridge, and Humpback Mountain in central Virginia; between Pine Grove Furnace State Park and PA 94 in Pennsylvania; and along the railroad tracks south of Dalton in Massachusetts.

CHICORY

Cichorium intybus

Because it is such a common plant—often considered just a weed in its habitat along roadsides, in waste places, and in open fields—Chicory is easy to overlook. Yet, of the plants found along the trail, its flower possesses a blue of the clearest kind. In his book, *A Countryman's Flowers*, Hal Borland was moved to say the flower was as "blue as the innocent eyes of a six-year-old."

The blossoms grow at intervals along the upper portion of the stem, opening early in the morning to entice passing bees and other insects. Yet, each flower lasts but a day. By early afternoon the petals have begun to wither, and they will have completely fallen off by the time darkness approaches. New blossoms will appear at different spots along the stem the next morning.

The early colonists imported Chicory from the Old World, where it had been cultivated as livestock feed for centuries. Turning it into a popular beverage, Egyptians harvested the plant from gardens along the Nile River more than five thousand years ago, and the Greeks who were contemporaries of Christ used it for medicinal purposes. Recent scientific investigations have found that the plant has antibacterial properties and that a substance in its roots can lower heart rates.

Chicory's leaves have been added to salads, while its roots have been dried and roasted as a substitute for, or an additive to, coffee. You will find an abundance of references to people enjoying Chicory coffee, but it is an acquired appreciation. The beverage is much stronger and quite a bit more bitter than the ground coffee most of us are used to buying in the supermarket.

Some places along the AT you are likely to encounter Chicory: Along VA 634 in southwest Virginia; near VA 42 road crossing in central Virginia; near Liberty Sod Farms in New Jersey; in the fields along Schaghticoke Road in Connecticut; and north of the Kennebec River in Maine.

MONKSHOOD

Aconitum uncinatum

FLOWER:

The Monkshood has one of the most eccentric shapes of any flower you will find along the trail. Of five irregular, petal-like sepals, the upper one forms a conspicuously rounded hood. This hood almost covers and hides two of the five smaller petals.

BLOOM SEASON:

August to October

LEAVES AND STEM:

The three- to five-lobed leaves are roughly toothed. Sometimes unable to hold the weight of its leaves and flowers, the two- to four-foot stem is often found leaning on other plants.

RANGE:

Georgia to Pennsylvania

If there ever was a plant that could live up to the title of "Pretty Poison," it would have to be the Monkshood. Notwithstanding its vivid purple tone and the intricate pattern of its delicate, florid sepals and petals, it is a highly toxic plant. While some references state that just its roots and seeds contain poisonous alkaloids, other sources admonish taking the slightest nibble from any part of the plant.

The toxicity found in members of the genus *Aconitum* was put to use for hundreds of years in the Old World. The Greeks and Romans dipped their spears and arrows into the juices of the plant, and others hid the roots inside bait to kill wolves (hence Monkshood's other common name of Wolfsbane).

Although the beauty of the plant has ensured its place in the flower gardens of Europe, authorities throughout the centuries have consistently warned against it. Writing in *A New Herbal* in the mid-1500s, William Turner exhorted, "This Wolf's bayne of all poysons is the most hastie poyson." In his 1629 work, *Paradisi in Sole, Paradisus Terrastris*, John Parkinson counsels "beware they come not near your tongue or lippes, lest they tell you to your cost, they are not so good as they seem to be."

Despite its negative attributes, early American settlers made a linament from the plant which would induce numbness and alleviate the pains of rheumatism. Modern medicine has found Monkshood to be useful as a sedative and in the treatment of sciatica and neuralgia.

Some places along the AT you are likely to encounter Monkshood: Close to Roan Highlands Shelter along the North Carolina–Tennessee border; and on Apple Orchard Mountain in central Virginia.

BOTTLE GENTIAN

Gentiana andrewsii

The Bottle Gentian, also called Closed Gentian, is a flower of the fall season, not appearing until late August and sometimes blooming well into October. The blossoms may even outlast those that are most often associated with autumn—daisies, asters, and goldenrods. *Gentiana clausa*, also known as Closed or Bottle Gentian, is nearly identical to *Gentiana andrewsii*, but its membranes do not extend above the petals, and its range is from Georgia/North Carolina to Maine.

The Bottle Gentians provide a wonderful illustration of the intricate workings of the natural world. Because the flowers remain closed, it takes considerable effort for an insect to work its way to the nectar. As a result, the plant is usually only visited by the largest and strongest of bees, but even they are hesitant to expend the energy unless they know they will be amply rewarded. Botanists have discovered that blossoms whose nectar has been harvested turn purple around their tips, while those still unvisited are marked with a bit of white to alert the bees that the sweet payoff still remains!

The species name of *andrewsii* honors Henry C. Andrew, well-respected in the 1800s for his wildflower paintings. The genus name comes from King Gentius, a ruler of the ancient country of Illyria (modern day Albania and Croatia), who supposedly discovered the medicinal uses of these plants. However, medical prescriptions for Gentian were found entombed with a mummy near Thebes, proving the ancient Egyptians knew of the medicinal properties at least one thousand years earlier.

Some places along the AT you are likely to encounter one of the Gentians: Between Little Hump and Hump Mountain along the North Carolina–Tennessee border; on Apple Orchard Mountain, on Tar Jacket Ridge, and between Salt Log Gap and Fish Hatchery Road in central Virginia; on the ridgeline just south of Milam Gap in Shenandoah National Park; and at Page Pond in New Hampshire.

GREEN FLOWERS

SKUNK CABBAGE

Symplocarpus foetidus

One of the earliest flowers to emerge from the ground to begin the annual floral season is Skunk Cabbage. If you want to find out how this unique-looking plant—which grows in moist woods and meadows—received its name, just rub it a bit and bring your hand up to your nose. Although Native Americans inhaled the aroma as a cure for headaches, once you take a sniff you probably won't want to do so again!

Because it sometimes blooms while February snows are still on the ground, the plant has developed a mechanism to withstand the cold. By burning carbohydrates stored in its large root system and produced from the cellular respiration resulting from its rapid growth, it is capable of producing its own heat—often melting the snow and ice around it. Temperatures inside its spathe have been found to be as much as twenty-seven degrees higher than the surrounding air.

Small gnats and flies inhabit the same marshy areas as the Skunk Cabbage and often emerge concurrently with the plant. Easily able to pass through the openings in each spathe, the insects are attracted to the beads of nectar on the tiny flowers, thereby ensuring pollination. Often, bees and other larger insects—which may have a hard time finding food in early spring—become trapped; they are able to push their way inside but are too large to escape back out of the opening.

Some places along the AT you are likely to encounter Skunk Cabbage: In wet areas on the trail paralleling the Blue Ridge Parkway in central Virginia and in Shenandoah National Park; near Fuller Lake in Pine Grove Furnace State Park in Pennsylvania; between Bear Mountain Bridge and Fahnestock State Park in New York; in the wet areas south of Blue Hill Road in Massachusetts; and between Beamis Stream and South Pond in Maine.

BLUE COHOSH

Caulophyllum thalictroides

FLOWER:

The small, half-inch, starry flowers of the Blue Cohosh (which can range from a yellowish green to a purplish brown) have six pointed sepals, six hooded glandlike petals, six stamens, and a single pistil. Though very small, they are conspicuous because they grow in branched clusters.

BLOOM SEASON:

April to June

LEAVES AND STEM:

About halfway up the stem, one to three feet in height, is a compound leaf that is divided into three lobes, with each lobe further divided into as many as nine leaflets. Just below the flower cluster is a smaller leaf with nine to twelve leaflets.

RANGE:

Georgia to Maine

Growing from rhizomes and native to rich, moist woods, the somewhat inconspicuous flowers of the Blue Cohosh often bloom before the leaves are fully open. At this early stage of development, the plant is covered in a waxy, bluish white tinge. The leafy foliage is reminiscent of the Meadow Rues, whose genus name of *Thalictrum* accounts for Blue Cohosh's species name of *thalictroides*.

The six stamens and one pistil of the flower mature at different rates, ensuring cross-pollination, while the petals have large nectar glands to attract the bees of early spring. The flowers are so small as to often be overlooked, so the plant is usually its most noticeable later in the year when it is adorned by pairs of what appear to be two dark blue grapes. These are, in actuality, the seeds that have grown through the fruit wall.

The plant has been known to cause skin rashes and can be quite irritating to mucous membranes. Although some sources point out that Blue Cohosh is poisonous, folklore has long held that, when roasted, the seeds are a good alternative to coffee. In addition, the plant is also commonly called Papoose Root, a reference to the fact that Native Americans and early settlers made a tea out of its root to induce menstruation as well as ease the pain of childbirth.

Some places along the AT you are likely to encounter Blue Cohosh: Thunder Hill and Dripping Rock in central Virginia; throughout Shenandoah National Park; on Day Mountain in Massachusetts; and near Velvet Rocks, and on Moose Mountain and Ore Hill in New Hampshire.

JACK-IN-THE-PULPIT

Arisaema triphyllum

Many people think the green, white, or purple sheath with a hood—the "pulpit"—that surrounds and covers "Jack" is the plant's flower. Actually, the sheath is just a leaf bract; in order to see the diminutive flowers, you need to lift up the hood and look inside. They are clustered around Jack's base. When you return in the fall, the "pulpit" will have fallen away and red berries will have replaced the flowers.

Jack-In-The-Pulpits are perennials that grow from corms, underground food-storage organs to which the roots are attached. From year to year the corm determines the sex of the flower. In times of abundant nutrients, the corm produces a female whose flower looks like small green berries surrounding the base of the column. If food is less bountiful, a male flower, resembling pollen-covered threads, results. Every once in awhile, a bisexual flower emerges, with the male components resting above the female parts. A Jack-In-The-Pulpit with only one leaf and no flower means the corm was basically starved for food during the previous year.

After putting the plant's roots through a rather elaborate cooking process, Native Americans pounded them into powder to be used as a type of flour. Hence, Jack-in-the-Pulpit's other common name, Indian Turnip. But don't try eating the root; without the Native Americans' methods of cooking, it is quite poisonous (containing calcium oxalate crystals).

Some places along the AT you are likely to encounter Jack-In-The-Pulpit: Between Wayah Gap and Nantahala River in North Carolina; south of Street Gap on the North Carolina–Tennessee border; on Pearis Mountain in southwest Virginia; on Sawtooth Ridge and Bald Knob in central Virginia; between Gravel Springs Gap and Thornton Gap in Shenandoah National Park; in wet areas between Lions Head and Bear Mountain in Connecticut; and on the lower slopes of the north side of Mount Greylock in Massachusetts.

FALSE HELLEBORE

Veratrum viride

FLOWER:
   False Hellebore's small, half-inch, star-shaped, greenish, hairy flowers grow in packed clusters at the top of the stem.
BLOOM SEASON:
   May to July
LEAVES AND STEM:
   The broadly oval, heavily ribbed leaves are six to twelve inches long, three to six inches wide, and are sessile with a clasping base.
RANGE:
   Georgia to Maine

Primarily found in damp environments—such as wet meadows, the edges of swamps and bogs, along stream banks, or on moist wooded slopes—False Hellebore is best observed from a distance; touching the plant can cause a severe skin irritation. Its foliage and rootstock have proven fatal to grazing livestock. One of its other common names, Indian Poke, may refer to the story that some chiefs of Native American tribes were permitted to ascend to that position only after they had survived eating the plant. A recent thru-hiker who mistook the plant for a Ramp (*Allim tricoccum*; see page 76) earned the trail name "Chief" Frodo after enduring a night of sweating, vomiting, and severe stomach cramps!

A substance found in False Hellebore has a tendency to reduce respiration and slow the heart rate. The plant was once used in medications, but since the appropriate dosage was hard to determine, a number of unintentional poisonings and overdoses occurred.

Many observers feel False Hellebore is at its most charming a short time before the flowers actually develop. As the large leaves begin to uncurl from around the stem, their undefiled yellowish green adds a welcome bit of color to the early spring forest. After the flowers have bloomed, the leaves deteriorate, turning brown and ragged-looking.

Small-Flowered False Hellebore (*Veratrum parviflorum*) may be found in drier environments along the AT from Georgia to Virginia. It is a smaller plant whose leaves are stalked and almost entirely basal.

Some places along the AT you are likely to encounter one of the False Hellebores: Between Chattahoochee Gap and Unicoi Gap in Georgia; between Siler Bald and Wayah Gap in North Carolina; between Spring Mountain Shelter and Little Bald on the North Carolina–Tennessee border; near Bryant Ridge in central Virginia; in wet areas on the slopes of Killington Peak in Vermont; and near Mizpah Spring Hut and south of Ethan Pond in New Hampshire.

RELATED OR SIMILAR SPECIES

WILD BLEEDING HEART
Dicentra eximia

SQUIRREL CORN
Dicentra canadensis

MIAMI MIST
Phacelia purshii

CATESBY'S TRILLIUM
Trillium catesbaei

PURPLE TRILLIUM
Trillium erectum

TOADSHADE TRILLIUM
Trillium sessile

VASEY'S TRILLIUM
Trillium vaseyi

TWISTED STALK
Streptopus roseus

SPOTTED WINTERGREEN
Chimaphila maculata

SHARP-LOBED HEPATICA
Hepatica acutiloba

FLAME AZALEA
Rhododendron calendulaceum

YELLOW LADY'S SLIPPER
Cypripedium calceolus

GREAT RHODODENDRON
Rhododendron maximum

ALPINE AZALEA
Loiseleuria procumbens

MOUNTAIN HOUSTONIA
Houstonia purpurea

FALSE FOXGLOVES
Aureolaria spp.

GLOSSARY

ANTHER: The part of the stamen containing the pollen.

AXIL: The (upper) point where the leaf and the stem meet.

BASAL: At the bottom of the stem.

BRACT: A modified leaf (which may be green or colored) growing near or below a flower.

CALYX: A term which collectively takes in the outer sepals.

COMPOUND: Divided into separate parts.

DOCTRINE OF SIGNATURES: The belief that whatever a plant looked like it could cure. For example, it is believed that members of the Snapdragon family are useful in treating throat sicknesses because of the mouth-and-throat form of the blossoms.

LANCEOLATE: Longer than it is broad, like the blade on a lance or spear.

OVATE: Shaped like an egg, with the base being wider than the tip.

PINNATE: A compound leaf whose leaflets are arranged along the main stalk (think of the way a feather is arranged).

PISTIL: A flower's female organ.

RACEME: A long stalk from which emanate a number of flowers growing on their own stems.

RHIZOME: A (usually) horizontal underground stem which has food stored in nodes and which sends up shoots.

ROSETTE: Refers to leaves which grow in a circular fashion at the base of a stem.

SEPAL: A modified leaf which surrounds the reproductive organs; collectively known as the calyx.

SESSILE: Has no stalk.

SPADIX: A thick stem on which are crowded many small flowers.

SPATHE: A leaf bract (or bracts) which enfolds or forms a hood around a spadix.

STAMEN: A flower's male organ.

STIGMA: The portion of the pistil (at its tip) which receives the pollen.

STIPULE: The tiny leaflike appendage (usually growing in pairs) at the base of the leaf stalk.

TERMINAL: Growing at the tip of the stem.

BIBLIOGRAPHY, SUGGESTED READINGS & FIELD GUIDES

Adams, Kevin, and Marty Casstevens. *Wildflowers of the Southern Appalachians: How to Photograph and Identify Them*. Winston-Salem, North Carolina: John F. Blair Publisher, 1996.

Adkins, Leonard M. *The Appalachian Trail: A Visitor's Companion*. Birmingham, Alabama: Menasha Ridge Press, 2000.

_____. *50 Hikes in Northern Virginia: Walks, Hikes, and Backpacks from the Allegheny Mountains to the Chesapeake Bay*. Woodstock, Vermont: Backcountry Publications, 2000.

_____. *Walking the Blue Ridge: A Guide to the Trails of the Blue Ridge Parkway*. Chapel Hill, North Carolina: University of North Carolina Press, 1996.

Alderman, J. Anthony. *Wildflowers of the Blue Ridge Parkway*. Chapel Hill, North Carolina: University of North Carolina Press, 1997.

Appalachian Trail Guides (a series of books covering the entire trail available from the Appalachian Trail Conservancy, Harper's Ferry, West Virginia).

Barnette, Martha. *A Garden of Words*. New York: Times Books, 1992.

Borland, Hal. *A Countryman's Flowers*. New York: Alfred A. Knopf, 1981.

Burn, Barbara. *North American Wildflowers*. New York: Gramercy Books, 1992.

Busch, Phyllis S. *Wildflowers and the Stories behind Their Names*. New York: Charles Scribner's Sons, 1977.

Catlin, David T. *A Naturalist's Blue Ridge Parkway*. Knoxville, Tennessee: University of Tennessee Press, 1984.

Coats, Alice M. *Flowers and Their Histories*. New York: McGraw Hill, 1971.

Dowden, Anne Ophelia T. *Look at a Flower*. New York: Thomas Y. Crowell Company, 1963.

Durant, Mary. *Who Named the Daisy? Who Named the Rose?*
New York: Dodd, Mead, and Company, 1976.

Eastman, John. *The Book of Forest and Thicket: Trees, Shrubs,
and Wildflowers of Eastern North America.* Mechanicsburg,
Pennsylvania: Stackpole Books, 1992.

Grimm, William Carey. *The Illustrated Book of Wildflowers
and Shrubs: The Comprehensive Field Guide to More than
13,000 Plants of Eastern North America.* Mechanicsburg,
Pennsylvania: Stackpole Books, 1993.

Gupton, Oscar W., and Fred C. Swope. *Fall Wildflowers of the
Blue Ridge and Great Smoky Mountains.* Charlottesville,
Virginia: University Press of Virginia, 1987.

_____. *Wildflowers of the Shenandoah Valley and Blue
Ridge Mountains.* Charlottesville, Virginia: University
Press of Virginia, 1979.

_____. *Wildflowers of Tidewater Virginia.* Charlottes-
ville, Virginia: University Press of Virginia, 1989.

Hatfield, Audrey Wynne. *Pleasures of Wild Plants.* New York:
Tangier Publishing Company, 1966.

Hersey, Jean. *The Woman's Day Book of Wildflowers.* New
York: Simon and Schuster, 1976.

Johnson, Charles W. *Bogs of the Northeast.* Hanover, New
Hampshire: University Press of New England, 1985.

Klimas, John E., and James A. Cunningham. *Wildflowers of
Eastern America.* New York: Alfred A. Knopf, 1974.

Lord, William. *Blue Ridge Parkway Guide: Rockfish Gap to
Grandfather Mountain.* Birmingham, Alabama: Menasha
Ridge Press, 1992.

Martin, Laura C. *Southern Wildflowers.* Marietta, Georgia:
Longstreet Press, 1989.

_____. *Wildflower Folklore.* Old Saybrook, Connect-
icut: Globe Pequot Press, 1984.

Niering, William A., and Nancy C. Olmstead. *National
Audubon Society Field Guide to North American Flowers:*

Eastern Region. New York: Alfred A. Knopf, 1995.

O'Brien, Bill, and Henry Edwards, eds. *The Appalachian Long Distance Hikers Association's Appalachian Trail Thru-Hiker's Companion.* Harper's Ferry, West Virginia: Appalachian Trail Conservancy, 2000.

Peterson, Roger Tory, and Margaret McKenny. *A Field Guide to Wildflowers: Northeastern/North-Central North America.* Boston: Houghton Mifflin Company, 1998.

Schaeffer, Elizabeth. *Dandelion, Pokeweed, and Goosefoot: How the Early Settlers Used Plants for Food, Medicine, and in the Home.* Reading, Massachusetts: Young Scott Books, 1972.

Stokes, Donald W. *The Natural History of Wild Shrubs and Vines: Eastern and Central North America.* New York: Harper and Row, 1981.

Weidensaul, Scott. *Mountains of the Heart: A Natural History of the Appalachians.* Golden, Colorado: Fulcrum Publishing, 1994.

The meetings and outings of local native plant societies are excellent places to learn more about wildflowers and make friends with people who share your interest.

GEORGIA NATIVE PLANT SOCIETY
P.O. Box 422085
Atlanta, GA 30342-2085
770-343-6000
www.gnps.org

TENNESSEE NATIVE PLANT SOCIETY
c/o Department of Botany
University of Tennessee
Knoxville, TN 37996

NORTH CAROLINA WILDFLOWER PRESERVATION SOCIETY
North Carolina Botanical Gardens
Totten Garden Center 3375
University of North Carolina
Chapel Hill, NC 27599-3375
www.ncwildflower.org

VIRGINIA NATIVE PLANT SOCIETY
400 Blandy Farm Lane, Unit 2
Boyce, VA 22610
540-837-1600
www.vnps.org

WEST VIRGINIA NATIVE PLANT SOCIETY
P.O. Box 808
New Haven, WV 25265-0808
www.wvnps.org

MARYLAND NATIVE PLANT SOCIETY
P.O. Box 4877
Silver Spring, MD 20914
www.mdflora.org

PENNSYLVANIA NATIVE PLANT SOCIETY
P.O. Box 281
State College, PA 19087
www.pawildflower.org

NATIVE PLANT SOCIETY OF NEW JERSEY
Office of Continuing Professional Education
Cook College
102 Ryders Lane
New Brunswick, NJ 08901-8519
www.npsnj.org

NEW YORK FLORA ASSOCIATION
3140 CEC
Albany, NY 12230
www.nyflora.org

ORGANIZATIONS

CONNECTICUT BOTANICAL SOCIETY
P.O. Box 9004
New Haven, CT 06532-0004
www.ct-botanical-society.org

NEW ENGLAND WILD FLOWER SOCIETY
180 Hemenway Road
Framingham, MA 01701-2699
508-877-7630
www.newfs.org

VERMONT CHAPTER, NEW ENGLAND WILD FLOWER SOCIETY
P.O. Box 2333
New London, NH 03257
www.newfs.org/vermont

NEW HAMPSHIRE CHAPTER, NEW ENGLAND WILD FLOWER SOCIETY
8 Boulters Cove
North Hampton, NH 03862
www.newfs.org/nh

JOSSELYN BOTANICAL SOCIETY
566 N. Auburn Road
Auburn, ME 04210

MAINE CHAPTER, NEW ENGLAND WILD FLOWER SOCIETY
Sawyers Island
RR 1, Box 79
Boothbay, ME 04537

JOE COOK hiked the Appalachian Trail in 1991 and 1992. A former newspaper photographer, he markets his nature/landscape photographs at galleries and art shows throughout the Southeast. He works for river protection organizations in Georgia.

MONICA COOK hiked portions of the Appalachian Trail in 1991 and 1992. She is currently managing catering and marketing for a restaurant in Rome, Georgia.

JOE AND MONICA are co-authors of *River Song: A Journey Down the Chattahoochee and Apalachicola Rivers*. Joe also photographed images for *Wildflowers of the Blue Ridge and Great Smoky Mountains*. They both live in Rome, Georgia, and have a daughter, Ramsey.

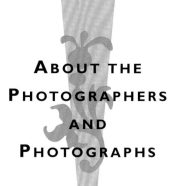

ABOUT THE PHOTOGRAPHERS AND PHOTOGRAPHS

The photographs in this book were shot during the course of two full years. Fujichrome 100 professional slide film was used exclusively. They were shot using a 35mm Nikon camera, employing on various occasions 50mm, 105mm and 180mm Nikon lenses as well as a Nikon No. 4T close-up filter. Natural light, in combination with a translucent plastic diffusion tent and hand held Photoflex light reflector, was used almost exclusively. On occasion, a Vivitar 283 flash unit was employed, as was a Kodak No. 81A warming filter and polarizing filter. A tripod was used for all exposures.

ABOUT THE AUTHOR

LEONARD M. ADKINS has been intimately involved with the Appalachian Trail for nearly two decades now. He has walked its full length four times and lacks less than six hundred miles toward completing it for a fifth time. He was a ridgerunner for the Appalachian Trail Conservancy and is presently an AT Natural Heritage Monitor, aiding the conference and the National Park Service in overseeing the welfare of rare and endangered plants. In addition, he currently serves on the Board of Directors for the Roanoke Appalachian Trail Club and maintains a section of the trail near McAfee Knob.

Among some of the other long-distance trails he has traversed are the Continental Divide Trail from Canada to Mexico, Canada's Great Divide Trail, and the Pyrenees High Route along the border of France and Spain. In all, he has hiked more than 16,000 miles exploring the backcountry of the United States, Canada, Europe, and the Caribbean.

Jobs as an interpreter for the Virginia State Parks system and as an assistant director for George Mason University's Outdoor Education Center helped increase his appreciation and knowledge of the natural world.

His works have received the National Outdoor Book Award, a Society of American Travel Writers Foundation's Lowell Thomas Travel Journalism Award, and one of *Foreward* magazine's Book of the Year Awards.

Along with his thru-hiking wife, Laurie, and thru-hiking dog, MacAfee of Knob, he lives in Catawba, Virginia—just one mile from the AT.